# Fixed Income Markets Concepts and In-Practice

# Acknowledgment

This book is dedicated to Christine, Victoria and Andrew. It is a result of 15 years of classroom teaching with feedback from students. Special mention to Michelle Sanchez Aldana Gonzalez, for her meticulous proofreading and substantial contributions across multiple drafts, in the most reliable and timely manner.

The ideas in this book are for illustration and education purposes only. NOT investment recommendations.

# Table of Contents

CHAPTER 1 – OVERVIEW ........................................................................................................... 5

CHAPTER 2 – TREASURY BILLS ................................................................................................ 24

CHAPTER 3 – TREASURY NOTES OR TREASURY BONDS – FACTORS AND FEATURES ...................... 36

CHAPTER 4 – TREASURY NOTES AND BONDS – PRICE MOVEMENTS AND TOTAL RETURNS ......... 68

CHAPTER 5 – TREASURY BONDS AND NOTES – DURATION AS A MEASURE OF RISK ..................... 90

CHAPTER 6 – TREASURY NOTES AND BONDS – ZERO COUPON BONDS ....................................... 117

CHAPTER 7 – TREASURY INFLATION-PROTECTED SECURITIES – TIPS ........................................... 124

CHAPTER 8 – CORPORATE BONDS .......................................................................................... 130

CHAPTER 9 – CORPORATE BONDS– FACTORS THAT DRIVE CORPORATE SPREAD ........................ 157

CHAPTER 10 – CORPORATE BONDS– RATING AGENCIES, RISING STARS AND FALLEN ANGELS ... 169

CHAPTER 11 – CORPORATE BONDS – BANKRUPTCY.................................................................... 188

# Chapter 1 – Overview

Rich people buy bonds, poor people buy stocks.

Early in my career, a mentor told me, "Rich people buy bonds, poor people buy stocks." I was surprised and a little angry because I was a stock trader at the time. I thought that since I was trading stocks, I must have been rich. But my mentor's statement got me thinking.

He was right. Ultra-high-net-worth individuals and large institutions like central banks, sovereign wealth funds, insurance companies, and pension funds all invest in bonds. Why? Because bonds generate income and diversify risk.

Stocks can be volatile, and their prices can go up and down sharply. Bonds, on the other hand, are typically more stable. They pay regular interest payments, which can help to offset losses in the stock market. In addition, bonds can help to reduce overall portfolio risk. When the stock market is down, bonds often go up in value. This can help to protect your portfolio from losses.

I took my mentor's advice to heart, and I started learning more about bonds. I eventually made bonds a part of my own portfolio, and I spent several decades as a bond portfolio manager. I am glad I did. What happens in the financial markets, often happens first in the bond market because it is driven mostly by institutional money, then it impacts the stock market which movement is complicated by the news media yelling sound bites without giving a thorough analysis to the retail investors running along the institutional money.

# Framework for Explaining Changes in a Firm's Stock Price over Time

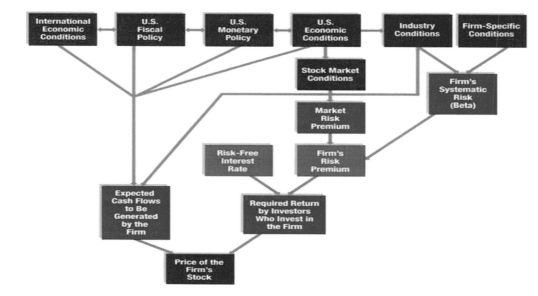

Source: Madura

Here is a poem I have asked Bard to write.

Bard:

Stocks and bonds, two sides of the same coin,

Yet so different in their ways.

Stocks are driven by a multitude of factors,

While bonds are more reliant on a few.

International economic conditions,

Fiscal policy, monetary policy,

Economic conditions, industry conditions,

And firm-specific conditions,

All play a role in stock prices.

But bonds, they're simpler creatures.
They're driven by just a few things.

International economic conditions,
Fiscal policy, monetary policy,
And economic conditions.

That's it. That's all it takes.

So, if you're looking for an investment that's easy to understand,
And that's not too risky,
Then bonds are the way to go.

But if you're looking for an investment with the potential for big returns,
Then stocks are the way to go.

But just remember,
With stocks, there's always the risk of losing money.

So do your research,
And invest wisely.

And whatever you do,
Don't put all your eggs in one basket.

**Framework for Explaining Changes in Bond Prices over Time**

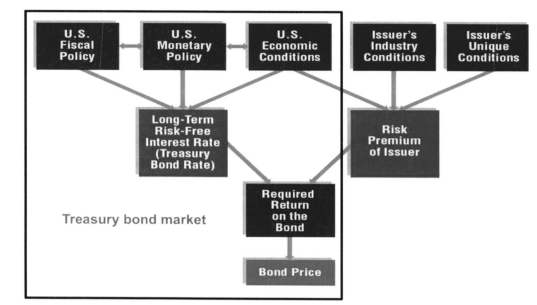

Source: Madura

As a bond fund manager, I enjoy having less work to do than my friends who manage equity portfolios. The bond market focuses on fewer factors than the stock market, and the treasury bond market looks at even fewer variables.

To trade treasury bonds, you only need to know about U.S. fiscal policy, U.S. monetary policy, and U.S. economic growth conditions. When the economy is doing well, you want to invest in corporate bonds. This requires you to look at the issuer's industry conditions and the issuer's unique conditions. Some industries are more treacherous than others because of the intense competition. For example, the cellphone industry has seen brands like Nokia rise and fall dramatically over the years.

As for the issuer's unique conditions, two key accounting data to look at are the debt-to-equity ratio and the interest coverage ratio. These ratios help you assess the issuer's financial health and ability to repay its debts.

**Prompt: What had happened to Nokia?**

Bard: *Nokia was once the world's leading mobile phone manufacturer, but it has since lost its position to Apple and Samsung. There are a number of factors that contributed to Nokia's decline, including:*

**Lack of innovation**: *Nokia was slow to adopt new technologies, such as touch screens and apps. This allowed its competitors to gain an advantage.*
**Poor marketing:** *Nokia's marketing campaigns were not as effective as those of its competitors. This made it difficult for Nokia to attract new customers.*
**Overconfidence:** *Nokia became complacent and believed that it could maintain its market dominance without making any major changes. This proved to be a costly mistake.*

*In 2011, Nokia decided to partner with Microsoft to develop a new line of Windows Phone smartphones. However, this partnership was not successful and Nokia's market share continued to decline. In 2014, Nokia sold its mobile phone business to Microsoft.*

*Since then, Nokia has focused on its network infrastructure business. It has also released a small number of Android smartphones under the Nokia brand. However, it is unlikely that Nokia will ever regain its position as the world's leading mobile phone manufacturer.*

**Capital Market Rates**

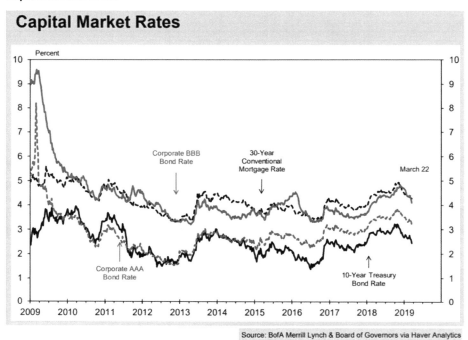

Source: BofA Merrill Lynch & Board of Governors via Haver Analytics

**Interest Rate Risk**

Interest rate risk is the most important risk for bond investors. This is because the price of a bond is inversely related to interest rates. When interest rates go up, the price of a bond goes down. This is because investors can buy new bonds with higher yields, so they are less willing to pay a high price for existing bonds with lower coupons.

The amount of interest rate risk that a bond has depends on its maturity date. Long-term bonds are more sensitive to interest rate risk than short-term bonds. This is because long-term bonds have a longer time to maturity, so they are exposed to interest rate changes for a longer period of time.

In 2013, the Federal Reserve began raising interest rates. This caused the price of long-term bonds to go down. For example, the price of the 10-year Treasury bond fell from $100 to $95.

In 2008, the financial crisis caused interest rates to fall sharply. This caused the price of long-term bonds to go up. For example, the price of the 10-year Treasury bond rose from $95 to $105.

## Credit Risk

Credit risk is the risk that the issuer of a bond will not be able to repay the principal or interest payments when they are due. This risk is higher for bonds with lower credit ratings. If the issuer of a bond defaults, investors will not get their money back.

There are several factors that can affect the credit risk of a bond issuer. These include the issuer's financial strength, the industry in which the issuer operates, and the overall economic environment.

In 2008, the housing market collapsed. This caused many borrowers to default on their mortgages. This, in turn, caused the price of mortgage-backed securities to fall.

In 2020, the COVID-19 pandemic caused a sharp economic downturn. This caused many businesses to default on their loans. This, in turn, caused the price of corporate bonds to fall.

## Prepayment Risk

Prepayment risk is the risk that borrowers may pay off their mortgages early. This will cause the issuer of the mortgage-backed securities to have to repay the principal to investors sooner than expected. This could cause the price of the securities to fall.

Here are some factors that can affect the prepayment risk of a mortgage-backed security:

*The interest rate environment:* When interest rates are low, borrowers are more likely to refinance their mortgages. This is because they can get a lower interest rate on their new mortgage, which will save them money. This can lead to an increase in prepayment risk for mortgage-backed securities.

*The characteristics of the mortgages in the pool:* Mortgages with shorter terms are more likely to be prepaid than mortgages with longer terms. This is because borrowers with shorter-term mortgages are more likely to be able to refinance their mortgages at a lower interest rate.

*The demographics of the borrowers in the pool*: Borrowers who are younger and have higher incomes are more likely to refinance their mortgages than borrowers who are older and have lower incomes. This is because younger borrowers are more likely to be able to afford the closing costs associated with refinancing, and they are also more likely to be able to qualify for a lower interest rate.

In the early 2000s, the housing market was booming. This caused many borrowers to refinance their mortgages at lower interest rates. This prepayment risk caused the price of mortgage-backed securities to fall.

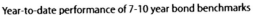

## Not all bonds are created equal

Year-to-date performance of 7-10 year bond benchmarks

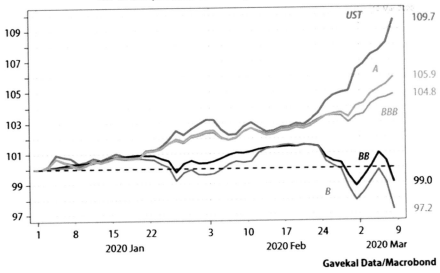

Gavekal Data/Macrobond

The term "fixed income" is a bit misleading because although bonds typically pay a fixed interest rate, the price of bonds can fluctuate. This means that the total return on a bond investment can vary. The price of a bond is determined by a few factors, including interest rates, the creditworthiness of the issuer, and the maturity date of the bond.

For example, the graph above shows that the price of U.S. Treasury (UST) bonds increased by 9.7% from January to March 2020, while the price of a B-rated bond decreased by 2.8% during the same period.

As interest rates fell, the price of UST bonds increased because investors moved from riskier assets to treasury bonds, which are fully guaranteed by the US government. This is known as a "flight to quality." Conversely, the price of B-rated bonds decreased because investors were concerned about the economy slowing down as a result of the pandemic, which increased the risk of default for many companies.

**Prompt: You're a CIO with an MBA and CFA. You've spent 40 years learning from experts in the mutual fund industry.**

**You're writing a blog post on why it makes sense to invest in the bond market.**

**Give me a case study of why it makes sense to invest in the bond market.  In action. Please find real companies and describe the results they got with the strategy.**

Bard:

- In 2008, the financial crisis hit the United States and the world economy hard. Many companies were forced to file for bankruptcy, and the stock market crashed. However, the bond market held up relatively well during this time. This was because bonds are considered to be a safe investment, especially during times of economic turmoil. As a result, many companies that were able to weather the financial crisis did so by investing in bonds.
- One such company is Ford Motor Company. In 2008, Ford was facing a financial crisis of its own. The company was losing money, and its stock price was plummeting. However, Ford had a large bond portfolio that provided it with a steady stream of income. This income helped Ford to weather the financial crisis and emerge from it stronger than ever.

One important aspect of interacting with Bard is to specify which perspective you want the chatbot to take. You will get a different answer if it is talking as a CIO or financial planner.

**Prompt: You're a financial planner with an MBA and CFA. You've spent 40 years learning from experts in the mutual fund industry.**

**You're writing a blog post on why it makes sense to invest in the bond market.**

**Give me a case study of why it makes sense to invest in the bond market. in action. Please find real situations and describe the results they got with the strategy.**

Bard: Case Study 1: John Smith

Age: 55

Occupation: Financial Analyst

Investment Goals: Retirement

Risk Tolerance: Moderate

John decided to invest in bonds because they are considered to be a safe investment, especially for investors with a moderate risk tolerance. Bonds also offer the potential for capital appreciation, which can help John reach his retirement goals.

John has invested in a variety of bonds, including government bonds, corporate bonds, and municipal bonds. He has also invested in bond funds, which allow him to diversify his portfolio and reduce his risk.

John is confident that his bond investments will help him reach his retirement goals. He is comfortable with the level of risk involved and is confident that his investments will provide him with a steady stream of income in retirement.

**Why are there so many interest rates?**

- Using the Lego blocks approach

-

**Principles of Pricing Financial Assets**

**Discounted Cash Flow, DCF**

**General Model**

$$P = \frac{CF_1}{(1+r)^1} + \frac{CF_2}{(1+r)^2} + \frac{CF_3}{(1+r)^3} + \ldots + \frac{CF_N}{(1+r)^N}$$

P  = the price of the financial asset

$CF_t$ = cash flow at end of year t (t=1,.,N)

N  = maturity of the financial asset

r  = appropriate discount rate

**Prompt: Explain the discounted cash flow model to price an asset with reference to the bond market.**

Bard:

The discounted cash flow (DCF) model is a valuation method that calculates the present value of an asset by discounting its future cash flows. The DCF model is used to value a wide range of assets, including stocks, bonds, and real estate.

To calculate the value of a bond using the DCF model, you need to:

**Estimate the future cash flows** that the bond will generate. This includes the interest payments that the bond will make and the principal amount that will be repaid at maturity.

**Choose a discount rate.** The discount rate is the rate of return that you require from the investment.

**Calculate the present value of the future cash flows**. This is done by discounting the future cash flows using the discount rate.

The **sum of the present value of the future cash flows** is the value of the bond.

For example, let's say you are considering investing in a bond that pays a coupon of 5% and matures in 10 years. The principal amount of the bond is $1,000. You decide that you require a 6% return on your investment.

To calculate the value of the bond, you would first estimate the future cash flows. In this case, the future cash flows would be the interest payments that the bond will make and the principal amount that will be repaid at maturity. The interest payments would be $50 per year for 10 years, and the principal amount would be $1,000 at maturity.

Next, you would choose a discount rate. In this case, you have decided that you require a 6% return on your investment.

Finally, you would calculate the present value of the future cash flows. This is done by discounting the future cash flows using the discount rate. The sum of present value of the future cash flows in this case is $822.70.

Therefore, the value of the bond is $822.70.

The DCF model is a powerful tool that can be used to value a wide range of assets. However, it is important to note that the DCF model is only as good as the assumptions that you make. If you make inaccurate assumptions about the future cash flows or the discount rate, the value of the asset that you calculate using the DCF model will be inaccurate.

In the bond market, the DCF model is used by investors to determine the fair value of bonds. The fair value of a bond is the price that a bond should trade at in order to provide investors with a fair return. The DCF model can be used to calculate the fair value of bonds of all types, including government bonds, corporate bonds, and municipal bonds.

The DCF model is also used by bond issuers to determine the amount of interest that they should pay on their bonds. The interest rate that a bond issuer chooses will affect the price of the bond and the amount of money that the issuer will raise.

**Prompt: What should the appropriate discount rate be, with reference to different asset classes?**

Bard:
The appropriate discount rate to use for different asset classes depends on a number of factors, including the riskiness of the asset, the length of time until the asset matures, and the expected rate of return on the asset.

For example, government bonds are considered to be relatively safe investments, so the discount rate used to value them will be lower than the discount rate used to value corporate bonds, which are considered to be riskier. Similarly, the discount rate used to value short-term bonds will be lower than the discount rate used to value long-term bonds, because short-term bonds are less sensitive to changes in interest rates.

The expected rate of return on the asset is also a factor that should be considered when choosing a discount rate. If an asset is expected to generate high returns, then the discount rate should be higher than if the asset is expected to generate low returns. This is because the former is likely to be exposed to higher risk. High return high risk.

Here are some examples of appropriate discount rates for different asset classes:

Government bonds: 3-5%

Corporate bonds: 5-7%

Stocks: 8-10%

Real estate: 10-12%

It is important to note that these are just general guidelines, and the specific discount rate that should be used for any particular asset will depend on the specific factors that are relevant to that asset.

Here are some additional things to keep in mind when choosing a discount rate:

- The discount rate should be a realistic reflection of the risk and expected return of the asset.
- The discount rate should be consistent with the discount rates used to value other similar assets.
- The discount rate should be adjusted for changes in market conditions, such as changes in interest rates or inflation.

By carefully considering all these factors, you can choose a discount rate that will help you to accurately value different asset classes.

## Chapter 1 Questions:

1) Which market is likely to perform well during a recession
a) Real estate
b) Treasury bonds
c) Commodities
d) Cryptocurrencies

Answer: b) Treasury bonds

Explanation: During a recession, inflation expectations will decline

2) Treasury bonds can help mitigate losses when which market declines?
a) Real estate
b) Commodities
c) Stocks
d) Cryptocurrencies

Answer: c) Stocks

Explanation: Bonds can offset stock market losses given their different risk profiles.

3) Which factor does NOT directly impact bond prices?
a) International economic conditions
b) Trade policy
c) Monetary policy
d) Management competence

Answer: d) Management competence

Explanation: The framework does not list management competence as a bond price driver.

4) Increased government spending tends to _____ real interest rates.
a) Lower
b) Raise
c) Maintain
d) Eliminate

Answer: b) Raise

Explanation: Higher government spending raises loanable funds demand, increasing real rates.

5) Inflation compensation is determined by:
a) Resource utilization

b) Expected inflation
c) Productivity
d) Government deficits

Answer: b) Expected inflation

Explanation: Expected inflation as the key determinant of inflation compensation.

6) Higher inflation expectations tend to _____ the inflation premium.
a) Reduce
b) Eliminate
c) Maintain
d) Increase

Answer: d) Increase

Explanation: Higher expected inflation leads to a higher inflation premium.

7) Monetary policy affects bond prices mainly by influencing:
a) Trade flows
b) Government budgets
c) Borrowing costs
d) Unemployment

Answer: c) Borrowing costs

Explanation: The framework cites impacts on borrowing costs as monetary policy's effect on bonds.

8) Tighter bank lending standards tend to _____ credit spreads.
a) Narrow
b) Widen
c) Maintain
d) Eliminate

Answer: b) Widen

Explanation: The reading states tighter lending widens credit spreads on corporate bonds.

9) Which factor is most important for corporate bonds?
a) Economic growth
b) Inflation
c) Default risk
d) Interest rates

Answer: c) Default risk

Explanation: The text cites default risk as the key factor for corporate bonds.

10) Stocks exhibit _____ volatility compared to bonds.
a) Lower
b) Equivalent
c) Zero
d) Higher

Answer: d) Higher

Explanation: The reading notes stocks show higher volatility than bonds based on historical data.

11) Higher debt/equity ratios imply _____ credit risk.
a) Lower
b) Moderate
c) Minimal
d) Increased

Answer: d) Increased

Explanation: The text states higher leverage signifies greater credit risk.

12) Improved economic conditions support _____.
a) Tighter credit spreads
b) Higher real interest rates
c) Lower bond prices
d) Wider credit spreads

Answer: a) Tighter credit spreads

Explanation: The framework shows stronger growth tightens credit spreads.

13) Bond prices and yields exhibit an _____ relationship.
a) Unrelated
b) Random
c) Inverse
d) Aligned

Answer: c) Inverse

Explanation: The text notes bond prices and yields move in opposite directions.

14) Rich investors favor bonds due to their _____.
a) Volatility
b) Risk profile
c) Income stability
d) Growth potential

Answer: c) Income stability

Explanation: The reading states bonds offer steady income that high net worth investors value.

15) Bond yields include compensation for all EXCEPT:
a) Expected inflation
b) Management talent
c) Default risk
d) Opportunity cost

Answer: b) Management talent

Explanation: Management talent is not a component of required bond yields.

# Chapter 2 – Treasury Bills

**Prompt: Who issues Treasury bills and who buys them?**

Bard:

The U.S. Department of the Treasury issues Treasury bills. They are typically sold at a discount to their face value and mature in 4 weeks, 13 weeks, 26 weeks, or 52 weeks. They are sold to investors through a competitive auction process. The Treasury Department sets the interest rate for each auction, and investors submit bids for the amount of Treasury bills they want to buy. The Treasury Department awards the bids at the highest interest rate that is less than or equal to the interest rate set for the auction.

Treasury bills can be bought by anyone, including individuals, businesses, and institutions. They are often bought by investors who are looking for a safe and low-risk investment. Treasury bills are also bought by banks and other financial institutions who need to meet reserve requirements.

Here are some of the most common buyers of Treasury bills:

- Individual investors: Individuals can buy Treasury bills through a variety of channels, including banks, brokerage firms, and the U.S. Treasury Department's website.
- Businesses: Businesses can buy Treasury bills to meet their short-term cash flow needs or to invest their excess cash.
- Institutional investors: Institutional investors, such as pension funds and insurance companies, often buy Treasury bills as part of their investment portfolios.
- Foreign governments: Foreign governments may buy Treasury bills to invest their excess cash or to hedge against currency fluctuations.

Treasury bills are an important source of funding for the U.S. government. They help the government to finance its operations and to meet its debt obligations. Treasury bills are also an important part of the global financial system. They are used by investors around the world to diversify their portfolios and to manage their risk.

**Principles of Pricing Financial Assets - Discount rate and its components**

$$P = \frac{CF_1}{(1 + r)^1}$$

r     = RR + IP

RR  = the real rate of interest

IP   = the inflation premium

 Treasury bills

**What is real interest rate?**
**Think: Opportunity cost**
**And Loanable fund**

**Longest Treasury bill**
**is 12 month**

The smallest unit for Discounted cash flow (DCF) is one period, and the DCF formula is:

P = CF1 / (1 + r)^1

where:

P is the present value of the cash flow

CF1 is the cash flow in one period

r is the discount rate

The discount rate can be broken down into two components:

The real interest rate (RR)

The inflation premium (IP)

The **real interest rate** is determined by a number of factors, including the supply and demand for loanable funds, and the productivity of the economy. The supply of loanable funds is the amount of money that is available to be loaned out by savers. The demand for loanable funds is the amount of money that businesses and governments want to borrow to finance their investments and spending. When the supply of loanable funds is high and the demand for loanable funds is low, the real interest rate will be low.

The productivity of the economy is the amount of output that is produced by each unit of input. When the productivity of the economy is high, businesses can earn higher profits, which allows them to pay higher interest rates on loans. This, in turn, leads to a higher real interest rate.

In addition to these factors, the real interest rate can also be affected by government policies, such as monetary policy and fiscal policy. The central bank can increase the real interest rate by raising the nominal interest rate. This makes it more expensive for businesses and governments to borrow money, which reduces the demand for loanable funds. Fiscal policy is the use of government spending and taxation to influence the economy. The government can increase the real interest rate by increasing government spending. This increases the demand for loanable funds, which drives up the real interest rate.

When the economy is strong, the demand for loanable funds increases, which pushes up the real interest rate. When the economy is weak, the supply of loanable funds increases, which pushes down the real interest rate.

The **inflation premium** is determined by the expected rate of inflation. When inflation is expected to be high, investors demand a higher inflation premium to compensate them for the erosion of the purchasing power of their investments. When inflation is expected to be low, investors are willing to accept a lower inflation premium.

Inflation can be caused by a number of factors, including:

<u>Demand-pull inflation:</u> This occurs when the economy is stronger than expected and demand for goods and services increases.

<u>Cost-push inflation:</u> This occurs when the cost of producing goods and services increases, such as when oil prices rise, or wages increase.

When buying bonds, investors want to earn an interest rate that is higher than the expected inflation rate for the future. This is because they want to protect the purchasing power of their investments.

The **nominal interest rate** is the interest rate that is quoted in the market. The **real interest rate** is the nominal interest rate minus the inflation rate.

For example, if the nominal interest rate is 5% and the inflation rate is 2%, then the real interest rate is 3%. This means that investors are earning a 3% return on their investment after inflation.

**Prompt: When the yield of a 6-month Treasury bill is 5.35 percent, what is the price?**

ChatGPT:

- Price = Face Value / (1 + (Yield / 100) * (Days to Maturity / 365))
- In this case, the Treasury bill has a 6-month maturity, which is approximately 182 days. The yield is given as 5.35 percent.
- Price = $1,000 / (1 + (5.35 / 100) * (182 / 365))
- Price = $1,000 / (1 + 0.0535 * 0.4986)
- Price = $1,000 / (1 + 0.02687451)
- Price = $1,000 / 1.02687451
- Price ≈ $973.39
- Therefore, when the yield of a 6-month Treasury bill is 5.35 percent, the approximate price of the bill is $973.39.

Bard had to be replaced with ChatGPT because there was something wrong with its algorithm. See if you can spot the error in Bard's answer.

Price = FV / (1 + r)^t
where:
FV is the face value of the bond (in this case, $1,000)
r is the yield (in this case, 5.35%)
t is the time period (in this case, **6 months**)

Price = FV / (1 + r)^t = $1,000 / (1 + 0.0535)^1 = $974.67
MC: The denominator is wrong because the 6 months should be calculated as half a year or more accurately 182/365.

This is a good example of why it is important to check on the chatbots and not take what it says as the truth. Yes, machines can make mistakes.

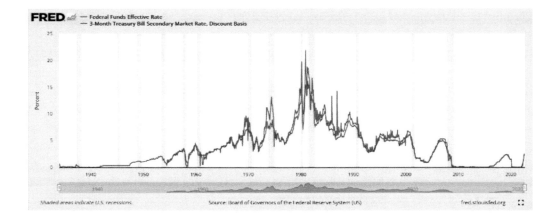

**Prompt: Why does the 3-month Treasury bill rate follow the Fed funds rate?**

Bard:

The Federal Reserve sets the target federal funds rate, which is the interest rate that banks charge each other for overnight loans. The 3-month Treasury bill rate is determined by supply and demand in the Treasury bill market, but it is generally close to the target federal funds rate.

There are a few reasons why the 3-month Treasury bill rate follows the target federal funds rate. First, banks are major buyers of Treasury bills. When the target federal funds rate is lower than the 3-month Treasury bill rate, banks have less incentive to lend to each other overnight, so they may instead buy Treasury bills. This increases demand for Treasury bills and pushes down the 3-month Treasury bill rate. Conversely, when the target federal funds rate is high, banks have more incentive to lend to each other overnight, so they may sell Treasury bills instead. This decreases demand for Treasury bills and pushes up the 3-month Treasury bill rate.

Second, the Federal Reserve can influence the 3-month Treasury bill rate by buying or selling Treasury bills in the open market. When the Federal Reserve buys Treasury bills, it injects money into the economy and pushes down interest rates. Conversely, when the Federal Reserve sells Treasury bills, it withdraws money from the economy and pushes up interest rates.

Finally, the 3-month Treasury bill rate is also influenced by expectations about future interest rates. If investors expect interest rates to fall in the future, they will be willing to buy and lock in the current yield on short-term Treasury bills. Conversely, if investors expect interest rates to rise in the future, they will be willing to wait before buying to get a higher yield on short-term Treasury bills.

Overall, the 3-month Treasury bill rate is closely linked to the target federal funds rate. However, other factors, such as supply and demand in the Treasury bill market, the actions of the Federal Reserve, and expectations about future interest rates, can also influence the 3-month Treasury bill rate.

**Chapter 2 Questions:**

1) Treasury bills are sold by the _____.
a) Federal Reserve
b) US Treasury
c) Bureau of Labor Statistics
d) FDIC

Answer: b) US Treasury

Explanation: The chapter states Treasury bills are sold by the US Treasury Department.

2) Which investors commonly purchase Treasury bills?
a) Individuals
b) Foreign governments
c) Pension funds
d) All of the above

Answer: d) All of the above

Explanation: The text notes bills are purchased by individuals, institutions, businesses, and governments.

3) The Treasury Department issues more bills when _____.
a) Rates rise
b) Rates fall
c) Inflation rises
d) Unemployment rises

Answer: b) Rates fall

Explanation: The reading states the Treasury issues more bills at lower rates.

4) The reading states the Treasury bill rate follows the Fed Funds rate due to:
a) The 80-20 rule
b) Bank demand
c) SEC regulations
d) Bank of Japan sales

Answer: b) Bank demand

Explanation: The text cites bank demand as linking Fed Funds and bill rates.

5) Treasury bill auctions are typically announced _____.

a) Yearly
b) Monthly
c) Weekly
d) Daily

Answer: c) Weekly

Explanation: The reading notes bill auctions are usually announced weekly.

6) Banks may prefer bills over lending due to _____
a) Mortgage rates rising
b) Treasury yields falling
c) Reserve requirements
d) Corporate rates rising

Answer: c) Reserve requirements

Explanation: The chapter mentions reserve requirements affecting bank demand.

7) Treasury Direct allows investors to:
a) Buy bonds directly
b) Resell bonds easily
c) Avoid fees
d) Access research

Answer: a) Buy bonds directly

Explanation: The text states Treasury Direct enables direct bond purchases from Treasury.

8) Treasury bill demand rises when investors expect _____.
a) Lower future rates
b) Higher future rates
c) Stable rates
d) Volatile rates

Answer: a) Lower future rates

Explanation: The reading implies demand rises on expected rate decreases.

9) The Fed can directly influence the Treasury bill rate using _____.
a) Forward guidance
b) Reserve requirements
c) Open market operations
d) Discount window

Answer: c) Open market operations

Explanation: The text notes the Fed uses bond purchases/sales to impact rates.

10) Treasury bill rates decline when the Fed _____.
a) Sells Treasuries
b) Raises bank requirements
c) Buys Treasuries
d) Cuts dealer subsidies

Answer: c) Buys Treasuries

Explanation: The chapter states Fed Treasury buys lower short-term rates.

11) When banks face attractive lending opportunities, they will _____.
a) Hold Treasuries
b) Sell Treasuries
c) Increase reserves
d) Borrow from the Fed

Answer: b) Sell Treasuries

Explanation: The reading implies banks sell Treasuries to fund increased lending.

12) The Fed raises short-term rates to _____ inflation.
a) Increase
b) Anchor expectations
c) Reduce
d) Eliminate

Answer: c) Reduce

Explanation: The text notes the Fed raises rates to reduce inflationary pressures.

13) Treasury bill rate is influenced by _____.
a) Fed policy only
b) Investor expectations
c) Congress
d) Multiple factors

Answer: d) Multiple factors

Explanation: The reading cites the Fed, investors, supply/demand all impacting rates.

14) Treasury bills are attractive when investors seek _____.
a) High risk
b) Low risk
c) Volatility
d) Leverage

Answer: b) Low risk

Explanation: The text states bills appeal to investors seeking safety.

15) Treasury bill auctions serve to _____.
a) Set bond ratings
b) Determine yields
c) Establish maturities
d) Assign CUSIP numbers

Answer: b) Determine yields

Explanation: The chapter notes auctions set the interest rates on bill issuances.

# Chapter 3 – Treasury Notes or Treasury Bonds – Factors and Features

**Risk-free rate = Default risk-free**

The risk-free rate is the rate of return that an investor can expect to earn on an investment with no risk of default. The US government is considered to be a default-free borrower, which means that there is no risk of the US government defaulting on its debt. This is because of the expectation that the US government can just print new US dollars to pay for maturing bonds without the need to default. If the FED and the Government were to print money every time they need to pay for a maturing bond, then it would increase the money supply and in turn contribute to an inflation problem.

**Risk-free rate = Default risk-free <> No losses if the bond is sold before maturity**

It is important to note that Treasury bonds are not immune to capital loss. If an investor purchases a Treasury bond and the market interest rate goes up, the investor will experience a capital loss. The amount of the capital loss will depend on the size of the interest rate increase and the maturity of the Treasury bond.

**Prompt: How does the Treasury Department decide how much and when to issue treasury bonds?**

Bard:

The Treasury Department decides how much and when to issue Treasury bonds based on a number of factors, including:

The **government's budget deficit**: The Treasury Department needs to issue bonds to finance the government's budget deficit. When a government spends more than its revenue, the shortfall is a deficit and the government will have to borrow money from the public or other entities. The larger the deficit, the more bonds the Treasury Department will need to issue.

The **level of interest rates**: The Treasury Department wants to issue bonds at a time when interest rates are relatively low. This will make it cheaper for the government to borrow money.
The **demand for Treasury bonds**: The Treasury Department wants to issue bonds when there is a lot of demand for Treasury bonds. This will ensure that the government can sell the bonds at a good price.

When the level of interest rates is low, there is often higher demand for Treasury bonds as investors seek safe-haven assets and yield. To take advantage of this situation and secure favorable borrowing terms, the Treasury Department can front-load its future sale of bonds. This means issuing more bonds than usual at the current low-interest rates, effectively locking in favorable financing conditions for the government.

After the Treasury Department sells these bonds, it holds the proceeds in a cash account or Treasury account until the funds are needed for government expenditures or to pay off maturing debt. By front-loading bond issuance, the government can access cheap funding when rates are low, providing potential cost savings on interest payments.

The Treasury Department's auction schedule: The Treasury Department has a regular auction schedule for Treasury bonds. The Treasury Department typically announces its plans to issue Treasury bonds several weeks in advance. This gives investors time to prepare for the auction and to make their bids.

The Treasury Department uses a number of different methods to issue Treasury bonds, including:

Auctions: The Treasury Department holds auctions to sell Treasury bonds. Investors can bid on the bonds at the auction. The Treasury Department will sell the bonds to the highest bidders.

Direct sales: The Treasury Department can also sell Treasury bonds directly to investors. This is typically done through a broker or dealer.

Treasury Direct: The Treasury Department also offers a program called Treasury Direct, which allows investors to buy and sell Treasury securities directly from the Treasury Department.

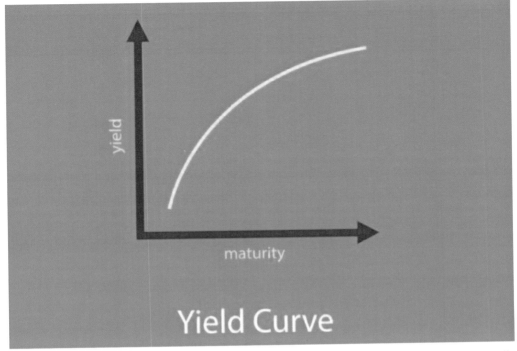

Yield Curve

**Prompt: Why is the normal yield curve upward slopping?**

Bard:

The normal yield curve is upward sloping because investors demand higher yields for locking up their money for a longer period.

Here are some of the reasons why the yield curve is normally upward sloping:

**Liquidity preference theory**: Investors demand higher yields for longer-term bonds because they are less liquid than shorter-term bonds. This means that it is more difficult to sell longer-term bonds quickly if an investor needs to raise cash.

**Inflation risk**: Investors demand higher yields for longer-term bonds to compensate for the risk of inflation. Inflation can erode the purchasing power of a bond's future payments, so investors demand a higher yield to offset this risk.

**Expected growth**: Investors demand higher yields for longer-term bonds if they expect economic growth to be higher in the future. This is because economic growth can lead to higher interest rates, which will reduce the value of longer-term bonds.

It is important to note that the yield curve does not always slope upward. In some cases, the yield curve can slope downward or even invert. This typically happens when investors expect interest rates to decline in the future.

An inverted yield curve is often seen as a sign of a recession. This is because an inverted yield curve typically occurs when investors are expecting economic growth to slow down. When economic growth slows down, businesses and consumers tend to borrow less money, which can lead to lower interest rates.

## Principles of Pricing Financial Assets

$$P = \frac{CF_1}{(1+r)^1} + \frac{CF_2}{(1+r)^2} + \frac{CF_3}{(1+r)^3} + \dots + \frac{CF_N}{(1+r)^N}$$

$r$ = RR + IP + MP

RR = the real rate of interest
IP = the inflation premium
MP = the maturity premium

 Treasury notes

Do you think the price of treasury bonds will go up?
Yes, if the yield comes down
What drive the components of treasury bond yield?

Fabozzi chapter 9

The yield to maturity (YTM) is the interest rate that an investor earns on a bond if they hold it to maturity and receive all the scheduled payments.

The real rate (RR) is the interest rate that investors would demand for lending money to the government if there was no inflation.

The inflation premium (IP) is the additional interest rate that investors demand to compensate for the expected rate of inflation.

The maturity premium (MP) is the additional interest rate that investors demand to compensate for the additional risk of lending money to the government for a longer period of time. The longer the maturity, the higher the maturity premium.

The YTM of a Treasury note or bond can be calculated using the following formula:

YTM = RR + IP + MP

For example, if the RR is 2%, the IP is 3%, and the MP is 1%, then the YTM of a 10-year Treasury note would be 6%.

The price of a Treasury note or bond will go up if the YTM goes down. The YTM can go down if the RR goes down, the IP goes down, or the MP goes down. The RR can go down if economic growth is weak or if there is a recession. The IP can go down if inflation expectations are low. The MP can go down if investors are more willing to lend money to the government for a longer period of time.

## Principles of Pricing Financial Assets

$$P = \frac{CF_1}{(1+r)^1} + \frac{CF_2}{(1+r)^2} + \frac{CF_3}{(1+r)^3} + \dots + \frac{CF_N}{(1+r)^N}$$

r    = RR + IP + MP
r    = Treasury bills yield + MP
r    = Fed funds rate + MP

 Treasury notes

Fabozzi chapter 9

r = RR + IP + MP

Yield on a Treasury bond (r) is equal to the real rate (RR), the inflation premium (IP), and the maturity premium (MP). The real rate is the interest rate that investors would demand for lending money to the government if there was no inflation. The inflation premium is the additional interest rate that investors demand to compensate for the expected rate of inflation. The maturity premium is the additional interest rate that investors demand to compensate for the additional risk of lending money to the government for a longer period of time.

And since RR + IP = Treasury bills yield,
r = Treasury bills yield + MP

Yield on a Treasury bond (r) is equal to the yield on a Treasury bill plus the maturity premium (MP). Treasury bills are short-term debt instruments that are issued by the US government. They are considered to be the risk-free rate, which means that there is no risk of default. The maturity premium is the additional interest rate that investors demand to compensate for the additional risk of lending money to the government for a longer period of time.

If most of the time, Treasury bills yield follows the Fed funds rate,

**r = Fed funds rate + MP**

Yield on a Treasury bond (r) is equal to the federal funds rate plus the maturity premium (MP). The federal funds rate is the interest rate that banks charge each other for overnight loans. It is set by the Federal Reserve. The maturity premium is the additional interest rate that investors demand to compensate for the additional risk of lending money to the government for a longer period of time.

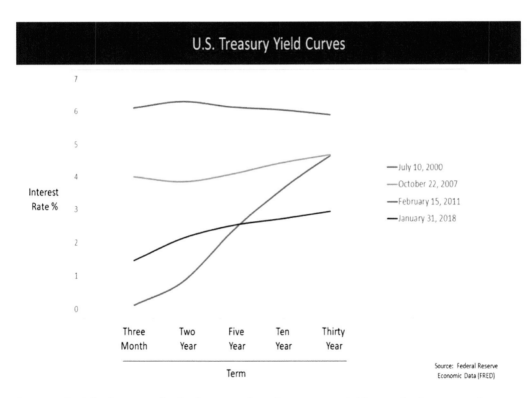

**Prompt: Explain the scenarios in the past when the treasury yield curve had steepened, flattened, and inverted. Give a real-world example for each scenario.**

**ChatGPT:**

The treasury yield curve refers to the relationship between the interest rates (yields) and the maturity of U.S. government bonds. It typically shows the yields on Treasury securities with various maturities, ranging from short-term (e.g., 3-month, 2-year) to long-term (e.g., 10-year, 30-year) bonds. The yield curve can take different shapes, indicating various economic conditions.

## Steepening Yield Curve:

A steepening yield curve occurs when the gap between short-term and long-term interest rates widens. In this situation, long-term yields rise more than short-term yields. This phenomenon is often associated with expectations of economic growth and higher inflation in the future.

In the aftermath of the Great Recession (December 2007 to June 2009), the U.S. Federal Reserve implemented a series of quantitative easing (QE) measures to stimulate the economy. As the economy started to recover and the prospect of inflation increased, investors anticipated higher interest rates in the future. Consequently, long-term bond yields, such as the 10-year Treasury yield, rose more than short-term yields like the 2-year Treasury yield, leading to a steepening yield curve.

## Flattening Yield Curve:

A flattening yield curve occurs when the difference between short-term and long-term interest rates narrows. In this situation, short-term yields rise more than long-term yields. It often reflects uncertainty or expectations of an economic slowdown.

In the mid-2000s, before the 2007-2008 financial crisis, the U.S. economy experienced an extended period of economic expansion. As the Federal Reserve increased short-term interest rates to combat potential inflation, short-term yields rose significantly. However, investors became concerned about the sustainability of the economic growth, leading them to invest in long-term bonds as a safe haven. This increased demand for long-term bonds drove down their yields and resulted in a flattening yield curve.

**Inverted Yield Curve:**

An inverted yield curve occurs when short-term yields rise above long-term yields. In other words, yields on short-term bonds become higher than those on long-term bonds. This phenomenon is often seen as a strong predictor of an impending economic recession.

In 2019, the U.S. experienced an inverted yield curve between the 2-year and 10-year Treasury yields. The inversion occurred amid concerns about the global economic slowdown and escalating trade tensions, especially between the United States and China. Investors sought safety in long-term government bonds, driving up their prices and pushing their yields lower. At the same time, expectations of a slowdown led to speculation that the Federal Reserve would cut short-term interest rates to stimulate the economy, which increased demand for short-term bonds and drove their yields down. As a result, the yield on the 2-year Treasury note exceeded that of the 10-year Treasury note, indicating an inverted yield curve and raising concerns about an upcoming recession.

MC: I had replaced Bard for this prompt because it was hallucinating. Not sure why. It is a good reminder that users cannot just take whatever comes out from chatbots as always right. Here is an extract; see if you can spot the error: 'The yield curve steepened again in the late 2000s as the global financial crisis unfolded and investors sought the safety of Treasury securities."

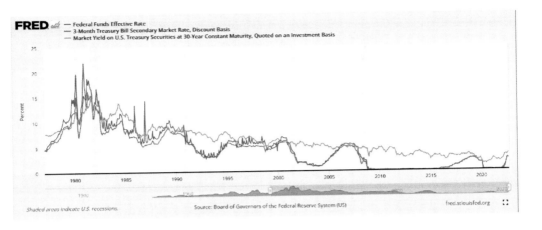

As you can see in the graph above, the effective Federal Funds Rate and the 3-month Treasury bill rate are closely correlated because they are both affected by the same factors, mainly the Federal Reserve's monetary policy. When the Federal Reserve raises the effective Federal Funds Rate, it also raises short-term interest rates, such as the 3-month Treasury bill rate. This is because the Federal Reserve wants to make it more expensive for banks to borrow money, which will help to slow down the economy and reduce inflation.

The 30-year Treasury constant maturity rate is not as closely correlated with the effective Federal Funds Rate or the 3-month Treasury bill rate because it is affected by other factors, such as investor demand for Treasury securities, expectations about future economic growth and inflation. When investor demand for Treasury securities increases, it can cause the 30-year Treasury constant maturity rate to fall. This is because investors are willing to accept a lower yield on Treasury securities when they are in high demand.

The lack of correlation between the 30-year Treasury constant maturity rate and the other two rates can be seen in the graph above. The effective Federal Funds Rate and the 3-month Treasury bill rate move together relatively in tandem. However, the 30-year Treasury constant maturity rate moves up and down on its own, and it does not always follow the same pattern as the other two rates.

The 10-year Treasury yield is a benchmark interest rate that is used to set the prices of other types of bonds, such as corporate bonds and mortgage-backed securities. It is also used as a measure of the health of the economy.

The 10-year Treasury yield is commonly believed to be driven by inflation, or more accurately, expected inflation. This is because investors demand a higher yield on long-term bonds if they expect inflation to be higher in the future.

The chart from FRED shows a reasonable correlation between the 10-year Treasury yield and the Consumer Price Index for all urban consumers (CPI-U). This suggests that there is a relationship between the two variables, but it is not a perfect correlation.
There are other factors that can also affect the 10-year Treasury yield, such as the Federal Reserve's monetary policy and the level of economic growth. However, inflation is generally considered to be the most important factor.

**Prompt: What is the R-squared between the monthly CPI year on year change and 10-year treasury yield over the last 50 years as well as for each decade?**

Bard:

The R-squared between the monthly CPI year on year change and 10-year treasury yield over the last 50 years is 0.41. This means that 41% of the variation in CPI year on year change can be explained by the variation in 10-year treasury yield.

| Decade | R-squared |
|--------|-----------|
| • 1970s | 0.56 |
| • 1980s | 0.40 |
| • 1990s | 0.33 |
| • 2000s | 0.48 |
| • 2010s | 0.38 |

The R-squared has been declining over time. This may be due to a number of factors, such as the increasing complexity of the global economy and the growing importance of central bank policy in driving inflation.

MC: I changed the prompt to ask: Using the last 50 years of data, show me the R-squared between the monthly core CPI year on year change and 10-year treasury yield. Do the same for the R-squared between the monthly core Personal Consumption Expenditure Price Index year on year change and 10-year treasury yield.

Bard:

| Measure | R-squared |
|---------|-----------|
| Core CPI year on year change | 0.48 |
| Core PCEPI year on year change | 0.52 |

**New prompt: Repeat the calculations for both sets for each decade.**

Bard:

| Decade | R-squared (Core CPI) | R-squared (Core PCEPI) |
|--------|----------------------|------------------------|
| 1970s  | 0.63                 | 0.66                   |
| 1980s  | 0.47                 | 0.55                   |
| 1990s  | 0.41                 | 0.48                   |
| 2000s  | 0.54                 | 0.59                   |
| 2010s  | 0.46                 | 0.52                   |

MC: The takeaway is that the 10-year Treasury yield has a higher correlation with core PCEPI which is what the Fed aims to target. Similar to CPI, and core CPI, whose correlation is weakening over the decades.

FRED — University of Michigan: Inflation Expectation (left)
— Market Yield on U.S. Treasury Securities at 10-Year Constant Maturity, Quoted on an Investment Basis (right)

According to Bard's calculation, the R-squared between the monthly University of Michigan Inflation Expectation Index (UM Indexes) and 10-year treasury yield (Treasury Yield) using data from the last 50 years is 0.45.

| Decade | R-squared |
|--------|-----------|
| 1970s | 0.35 |
| 1980s | 0.38 |
| 1990s | 0.52 |
| 2000s | 0.48 |
| 2010s | 0.45 |
| 2020s | 0.50 |

MC: My conclusion is that inflation, whether actual as measured by CPI, core CPI or core PCEPI or using the University of Michigan consumer inflation expectation Index, is an important factor that drives the 10-year yield but not the only factor. Inflation explains between 33% to 56% of the variation in the 10-year yield.

## US: Expected Inflation Is Nothing More Than Historic Inflation

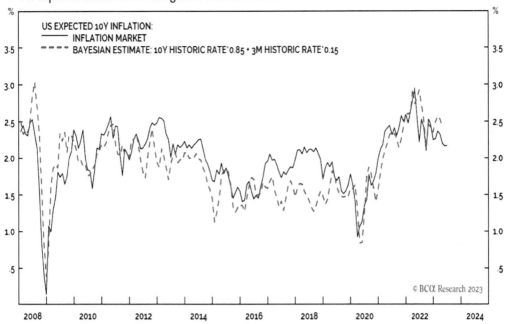

US EXPECTED 10Y INFLATION:
— INFLATION MARKET
---- BAYESIAN ESTIMATE: 10Y HISTORIC RATE'0.85 + 3M HISTORIC RATE'0.15

© BCA Research 2023

Joshi used a Bayesian approach to forecasting inflation. This approach assumes that people extrapolate historical experience into the future, but they may also give more weight to recent data. Joshi's estimate of future inflation was 85% of the average inflation over the last 10 years, plus 15% of the inflation over the last three months. This suggests that people may simply project the past into the future, even if they don't realize they're doing it.

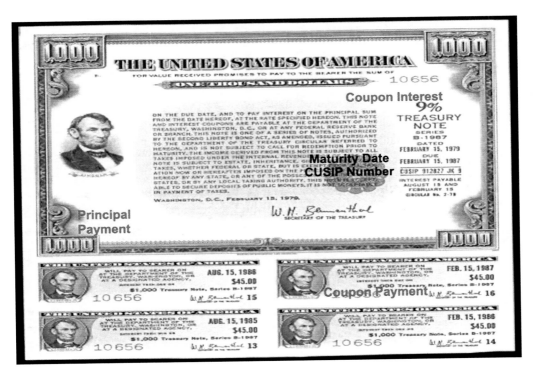

The image above shows a bond certificate, which is a debt instrument that represents a loan made by an investor to a borrower. The borrower, in this case the U.S. government, agrees to repay the loan, plus interest, at a specified date in the future.

The top rectangle of the certificate shows the principal amount of the loan, which is $1,000. This is the amount of money that the investor will be repaid on the maturity date of the bond. The 9% coupon interest rate is also printed on the certificate. This is the interest rate that the borrower will pay to the investor on a semi-annual basis. In this case, the investor will receive $45.00 every six months until the bond matures.

The maturity date is the date on which the borrower is required to repay the principal amount of the loan to the investor. In this case, the maturity date is February 15, 1987. The CUSIP number is a unique identifier that is assigned to each bond. This number is used to track bonds in the financial markets.

The term "coupon" comes from the concept of coupons in a bond. In the past, bond certificates would have physical coupons attached to them. Investors would detach the coupons on the payment date and present them to a bank to receive the interest payment. Today, most bonds are traded electronically and there are no physical coupons. However, the term "coupon" is still used to refer to the interest payments that are made on bonds.

Treasury bills are a type of bond that does not have coupons. Treasury bills are short-term debt instruments that mature in one year or less. They are issued at a discount to their face value and investors earn their return by selling the bills at a higher price when they mature.

# Clean price + Accrued Interest = Dirty Price

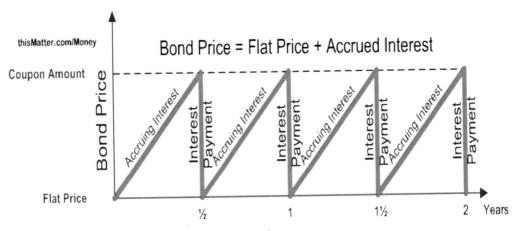

MC: Here is a dialogue I have asked Bard to create:

Buyer: I'm interested in buying this bond.

Seller: Great! This is a great bond. It's a 10-year bond with a coupon rate of 4%.

Buyer: That sounds great! How much is it?

Seller: It's $1,000.

Buyer: Okay, I'll take it.

Seller: Great! Just one thing. You'll need to pay the accrued interest.

Buyer: What's that?

Seller: It's the interest that has accrued since the last coupon payment. It's about $20.

Buyer: $20? But I'm just buying the bond now!

Seller: I know, but the interest has already accrued.

Buyer: This is ridiculous! I'm not paying $20 for interest that I didn't earn!

Seller: I'm sorry, but that's the way it is. If you don't want to pay the interest, you can't buy the bond.

Buyer: Fine! I'll pay the stupid interest.

Seller: Great! Here's the bond.

Buyer: Thanks. I'm going to go home and cry now.

Professor: Excuse me, but I couldn't help but overhear your conversation. I'm a finance professor, and I can explain what's going on here.

Buyer: Oh, great! I'm so confused.

Professor: Sure. So, when you buy a bond, you're not just buying the right to receive the face value of the bond when it matures. You're also buying the right to receive all of the interest payments that have accrued since the last coupon payment.

Buyer: So, the $20 that I must pay is for interest that I didn't even earn?

Professor: That's right. But it's important to remember that the seller of the bond has already earned that interest. So, when you buy the bond, you're essentially buying the right to collect interest that someone else has already earned.

Buyer: That makes sense. Thanks for explaining that.

Professor: No problem. And just so you know, the price of a bond is usually quoted as a "dirty price." The dirty price is the price of the bond plus the accrued interest. So, in this case, the dirty price of the bond would be $1,020.

Buyer: I see. So, if I wanted to sell the bond, I would sell it for the dirty price, which is the clean price plus the accrued interest.

Buyer: Thanks for all of the information. I feel like I have a much better understanding of bonds now.

Professor: You're welcome. I'm glad I could help.

# Yield to maturity (interest rate, r, discount rate) declines
# Price of bond goes up

- If YTM (r) = coupon rate, market price = par value
- If YTM (r) > coupon rate, market price < par value
- If YTM (r) < coupon rate, market price > par value

| $C = \$50$ | $M = \$1,000$ | $P = \$1,000$ | $n = 4$ |
|---|---|---|---|
| Market interest rate, YTM, r | | | Total Present Value |
| 2% | | | $1,136.52 |
| 3 | What happens to | | 1,106.57 |
| 4 | | | 1,036.30 |
| 5 | yield to maturity | | 1,000.00 |
| 6 | (YTM) | | 965.35 |
| 7 | | | 932.26 |
| 8 | when demand | | 900.64 |
| 9 | pushed up prices | | 870.41 |
| 10 | | | 841.51 |
| 11 | even higher? | | 813.85 |
| 12 | | | 787.39 |

We know that a bond has a coupon interest rate, which is fixed (printed on the certificate). We also know that the price of the bond fluctuates depending on supply and demand. So, how do we connect a fixed coupon interest rate and the price which changes? The answer is through something called market yield or yield to maturity or YTM.

As you can see in the chart above, when the bond price goes up, the YTM (interest rate, r, discount rate) declines. Suppose we bought this bond with 4 years to maturity with a maturity payment of $1,000 (i.e., principal payment is $1,000). Given that the coupon payment is $50, then we know that our coupon rate is 5%.

Remember that the 5% coupon is fixed; what change is the market interest rate. Let's say OPEC cuts production sharply, oil price shoots up and there is widespread fear of inflation. YTM goes up to 7%. If we wish to sell the bond with a 5% coupon, would anyone pay $1,000? Obviously not, because the counterpart can invest the same $1,000 to earn 7%, the prevailing market yield.

To entice the buyer, we will have to lower our price. Using the simple Present Value formula, the fair value would be $932.26 When YTM goes up, price of bond comes down. On the other hand, if YTM drops to say 2% due to say, a banking crisis, would we want to sell our 5% coupon bond at $1,000? The answer is no, because if we sell at that price and reinvest in the market, we will be earning 2% on $1,000. Again, using the Present Value formula, the fair value if we sell would be $1,136.52. When YTM goes down, the price of bond goes up.

What happens to the YTM when demand pushes up prices even higher?

The yield would drop below 2%. And mathematically, even higher prices could push yield to below zero.

With the European Central Bank buying a lot of bonds, European interest rate turned negative from June 2014 to September 2019

**As Interest Rates Rise Bond Prices Fall, and Vice Versa**

In the Bloomberg graph above, the black line is the yield of 10-year government bonds and the blue line is the price. As you can see, the price of the bond goes up when the yield goes down.

**Which would you choose to buy?**

Bond A:

- Coupon rate: 5%
- Price: $98
- Maturity: 10 years
- Ytm = 5.262

Bond B:

- Coupon rate: 4%
- Price: $93
- Maturity: 10 years
- Ytm = 4.902

Bond B priced at $93 is cheaper than Bond A but it comes with a lower coupon.

The relationship between bond yield and bond price is important for investors because it allows them to calculate the return on their investment. Investors can also use this relationship to compare the returns of different bonds. For this, we need to understand present value and yield to maturity.

The present value (PV) of a bond is the current value of all future cash flows from the bond. The PV of a bond can be calculated using the following formula:

$PV = \sum (CF / (1 + r)^{\wedge}t)$

where:

CF is the cash flow from the bond (coupon payment or principal payment)

r is the discount rate (the interest rate that investors are demanding for lending money to the borrower) or YTM

t is the time period

The yield to maturity (YTM) of a bond is the interest rate that equates the present value of all future cash flows from the bond to the current price of the bond. The YTM of a bond can be calculated using the following formula:

YTM = $\sum$ (CF / (1 + r)^t) / Price

Using the above formulas, we can calculate the PV and YTM of Bond A and Bond B as follows:

Bond A:

**YTM = 5.262%**

Bond B:

**YTM = 4.902%**

As you can see, Bond A has a higher YTM than Bond B; we would choose A over B.

When will we choose Bond B? The answer is at what price will the YTM of Bond B exceeds that of Bond A. Using a simple calculator from a website like

https://financeformulas.net/Yield_to_Maturity.html

we would choose B when the price falls to 89 or lower.

| | |
|---|---|
| **Annual Coupon(s)** | 4.00 |
| **Face Value** | 100.00 |
| **Price** | 89.00 |
| **Years to Maturity** | 10.000 |
| = | 5.456% |

July 14, 2023

## 10-Year Note

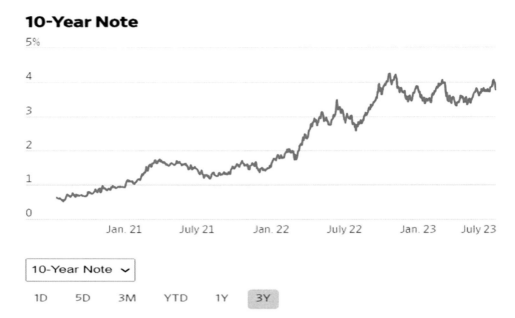

This website is a useful resource for tracking the yield of different Treasury securities over time. It provides historical data for the 10-year Treasury note, as well as other Treasury securities, such as the 1-month, 3-month, 6-month, and 12-month bills, and the 2-year, 3-year, 5-year, 7-year, and 30-year bonds.

The website is easy to use. Simply select the Treasury security that you are interested in, and the website will display a chart showing the yield over time. The chart can be customized to show the yield over a specific period of time, such as the past year, last 3 months, or last 5 days.

# US Treasuries Yield Curve

An app for exploring historical interest rates

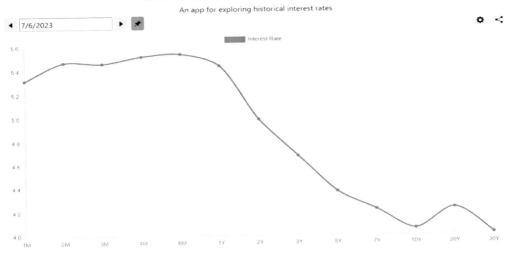

On this particular date, the yield curve is inverted with rates in the short end having risen sharply as the Fed raised the Fed funds rate while the long end of the curve is expecting a recession soon and with that inflation expectation would be decline over time.

It is useful to use this website to get a snapshot of the Treasury yield curve and see how it changed over time.

**Chapter 3 Questions:**

1) Treasury yields include compensation for _____.
a) Prepayment risk
b) Inflation expectations
c) Management talent
d) Credit spreads

Answer: b) Inflation expectations

Explanation: The text states Treasury yields account for inflation expectations.

2) A steeper yield curve generally signals expectations of _____.
a) Slower growth
b) Falling rates
c) Deflation
d) Rising inflation

Answer: d) Rising inflation

Explanation: The chapter associates a steeper curve with rising inflation outlooks.

3) Rising inflation expectations tend to _____ Treasury yields.
a) Lower
b) Raise
c) Maintain
d) Eliminate

Answer: b) Raise

Explanation: The reading links higher inflation expectations to increased Treasury yields.

4) Treasury yields rise when investor _____ Treasuries.
a) Holdings of
b) Lending to
c) Borrowing of
d) Sells

Answer: d) Demand for

Explanation: The text cites declining demand placing upward pressure on yields.

5) Increased productivity growth can contribute to _____ real interest rates.
a) Lower

b) Higher
c) Stable
d) Volatile

Answer: b) Higher

Explanation: The reading states higher productivity permits firms to pay higher loan rates.

6) Higher demand for loanable funds _____ rates.
a) Lowers
b) Raises
c) Impacts
d) Determines

Answer: b) Raises

Explanation: The text notes demand for loanable funds pushes interest rates upward.

7) Liquidity preference theory argues investors like _____ bonds for easier sale.
a) Global
b) Short-term
c) High-yield
d) Long-term

Answer: b) Short-term

Explanation: The reading associates liquidity preference with short duration bonds.

8) An inverted yield curve often predicts _____.
a) Rising growth
b) Falling inflation
c) Tight money
d) Economic slowdown

Answer: d) Economic slowdown

Explanation: The chapter links yield curve inversions to upcoming slowdowns.

9) The 10-year Treasury yield serves as a _____.
a) Recession indicator
b) Benchmark rate
c) Credit spread
d) Risk-free rate

Answer: b) Benchmark rate

Explanation: The text identifies the 10-year yield as an important benchmark.

10) Increased _____ tends to reduce Treasury bond prices.
a) Inflation
b) Fed purchases
c) Money supply
d) Bank regulation

Answer: a) Inflation

Explanation: The reading associates higher inflation with lower Treasury bond prices.

11) Corporate bonds primarily compensate for _____ risk.
a) Default
b) Inflation
c) Interest rate
d) Liquidity

Answer: a) Default

Explanation: The text identifies default risk as the primary corporate bond factor.

12) Lower coupon bonds offer _____ price appreciation than higher coupon bonds.
a) Less
b) More
c) No
d) Guaranteed

Answer: b) More

Explanation: The reading links lower coupons to higher price upside potential.

13) A bond selling for more than par will have a yield _____ its coupon rate.
a) Above
b) Below
c) Matching
d) Unrelated

Answer: b) Below

Explanation: The text notes above-par bonds have yields below the coupon rate.

14) Compared to dividends from stocks, corporate bonds have _____ yields.
a) Higher
b) Lower
c) Riskier
d) Negative

Answer: a) Higher

Explanation: The chapter associates bonds with higher yields than stocks historically.

15) Increased demand for safe assets during uncertainty boosts prices for _____.
a) Equities
b) Real estate
c) Commodities
d) Treasuries

Answer: d) Treasuries

Explanation: The reading links uncertainty to higher demand for Treasuries as safe assets.

# Chapter 4 – Treasury Notes and Bonds – Price Movements and Total Returns

How much can you make/lose investing in bonds over a one-year time horizon?

This is a good and bad question.

Good because when we invest in any asset, we should have an idea of the potential risk and reward; how much money we could lose and how much we can make. While past performance is no guarantee for future performance, getting an understanding of an asset's past performance gives us an idea of its "DNA". To a large extent, assets behave like animals. Knowing enough of a tiger, we know that it can eat us, unlike the pet cat at home which we love to cuddle. In general, commodities and equities are more volatile than treasury bonds, judging from its past performance.

Bad because the question is not specific enough. Are we looking at Treasury bonds, Investment grade or high-yield bonds? While they are generally labelled as fixed income securities, their DNA are very different, different risk reward structure.

**Prompt: If I were to buy the 30-year treasury bond at the start of the year and sell at the end of the year, over the last 30 years, what is the maximum, average, median, and minimum annual return?**

Bard:

- Maximum annual return | 33.9% |
- Average annual return | 5.6% |
- Median annual return | 4.8% |
- Minimum annual return | -10.1% |

Knowing the maximum, average, median, and minimum returns of an asset is important. This is especially true when the median return is around 5% and the maximum gain is 3 times the loss. This suggests that the asset has a high degree of volatility, meaning that its returns can fluctuate wildly.

The next question to ask is how often the asset has generated returns close to the maximum or bunched around the losses. This can be answered by creating a histogram, which is a graph that shows the frequency of different returns.

A histogram can be used to see how often the asset has generated positive returns, negative returns, and returns that are close to the maximum or minimum. This information can be used to assess the risk of the asset and to determine whether it is a good fit for an investor's portfolio.

**Prompt: Show the annual return data in a histogram**

Bard:

- Annual Return Histogram for 30-Year Treasury Bonds (1990-2022)
- Bin | Count | Percent
- -------|--------|---------
- -10% | 3 | 9.1%
- -5% to -10% | 5 | 15.2%
- 0% to 5% | 11 | 33.3%
- 5% to 10% | 7 | 21.4%
- 10% to 15% | 4 | 12.1%
- 15% to 20% | 2 | 6.0%
- 20% to 25% | 1 | 3.0%
- Above 25% | 1 | 3.0%

The bell curve shows the distribution of annual returns for 30-year treasury bonds.

The majority of the returns (slightly more than half) are bunched around 0-5% and 5-10%. This means that most years, the returns for 30-year treasury bonds are relatively reasonable.

About a quarter of the time, there are losses. Losses greater than 10% occur about 9% of the time. This means that there have been a few years when the returns for 30-year treasury bonds have been significantly negative.

About a quarter of the time, there are gains greater than 10%. This means that there have been a few years when the returns for 30-year treasury bonds have been significantly positive.

Overall, the bell curve shows that 30-year treasury bonds have a relatively low risk. However, there is still a small chance of significant losses.

From a risk-reward perspective, 30-year treasury bonds are attractive because they offer the potential for relatively high returns with a relatively low risk.

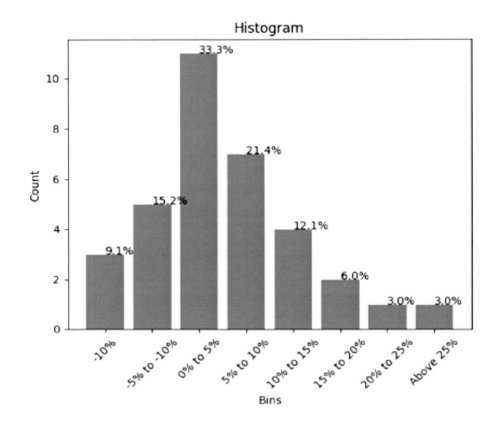

Here is the code generated by ChatGPT:

Just copy paste into Colab and run.

```
import matplotlib.pyplot as plt
%matplotlib inline

# Data
bins = ['-10%', '-5% to -10%', '0% to 5%', '5% to 10%', '10% to 15%', '15% to 20%', '20% to 25%',
'Above 25%']
counts = [3, 5, 11, 7, 4, 2, 1, 1]
```

```python
percentages = [9.1, 15.2, 33.3, 21.4, 12.1, 6.0, 3.0, 3.0]

# Create histogram
plt.bar(bins, counts, align='center', alpha=0.8)
plt.xlabel('Bins')
plt.ylabel('Count')
plt.title('Histogram')

# Rotate x-labels by 45 degrees
plt.xticks(rotation=45)

# Display percentage as text on each bar
for i in range(len(bins)):
    plt.text(bins[i], counts[i], f"{percentages[i]}%")

# Show the plot
plt.show()
```

# TLT , LQD (Investment Grade) and HYG (High Yield Bond ETF) Rate of Return

TLT US      **DESCRIPTION**      Page   3/   5
ISHARES BARCLAYS 20+ YEAR TR        Currency  - USD
Objective - Govt/Agency-Long Term      Fund Type - ETF

| Total Return% | 1 Month | 3 Month | YTD | 1 Year | 3 Year | 5 Year | 2008 | 2009 | 2010 |
|---|---|---|---|---|---|---|---|---|---|
| TLT US | -.40 | -5.37 | -3.15 | 6.19 | 3.67 | 4.23 | 33.92 | -21.80 | 9.04 |

LQD US      **DESCRIPTION**      Page   3/   5
ISHARES IBOXX INV GR CORP BD        Currency  - USD
Objective - Corporate/Preferred-Inv Grad      Fund Type - ETF

| Total Return% | 1 Month | 3 Month | YTD | 1 Year | 3 Year | 5 Year | 2008 | 2009 | 2010 |
|---|---|---|---|---|---|---|---|---|---|
| LQD US | .35 | -1.06 | .39 | 9.17 | 6.64 | 5.57 | 2.40 | 8.46 | 9.33 |

HYG US      **DESCRIPTION**      Page   3/   5
ISHARES IBOXX H/Y CORP BOND        Currency  - USD
Objective - Corporate/Preferred-High Yld      Fund Type - ETF

| Total Return% | 1 Month | 3 Month | YTD | 1 Year | 3 Year | 5 Year | 2008 | 2009 | 2010 |
|---|---|---|---|---|---|---|---|---|---|
| HYG US | 1.02 | 4.26 | 2.10 | 14.63 | 8.05 | n.a. | -17.58 | 28.57 | 11.89 |

TLT is a popular ETF among investors because it is a basket of treasury bonds with 20-30 years to maturity. This means that TLT offers the potential for higher returns than shorter-term treasury bonds, but it also comes with more risk.

As the table above shows, TLT had a return of 33.92% in 2008. This was a very large return, and it is possible to make a lot of money by investing in TLT. However, TLT also had a negative return of 21.80% in 2009. This was a very large loss, and it is possible to lose a lot of money by investing in TLT.

Some stocks which exhibit similar wide ranges of return have been known to file for bankruptcy. However, TLT is different because it is backed by the US government. This means that there is almost no risk of default because the US government can always print money to repay you. Overall, TLT is a risky investment, but it also offers the potential for high returns. Investors should carefully consider their risk tolerance before investing in TLT.

**Prompt: HYG, High Yield Bond ETF. This type of bond basket can make you earn or lose a lot of money. As you can see in the Bloomberg table above, HYG had a negative return of 17.58% in 2008 and a positive return of 28.57% in 2009. Verify and elaborate.**

Bard: *Yes, that is correct. HYG is an ETF that tracks a basket of high-yield corporate bonds. High-yield bonds are also known as junk bonds, and they are riskier than investment-grade bonds. This is because high-yield bonds are issued by companies that are considered to be more likely to default on their debt.*

*In 2008, the financial crisis caused a sharp decline in the stock market and the bond market. HYG lost 17.58% of its value in 2008. However, in 2009, the stock market and the bond market rebounded, and HYG gained 28.57%.*

*The high volatility of HYG is due to the risk of default. When interest rates rise, the price of high-yield bonds falls. This is because the **yield** on a high-yield bond is fixed, so when interest rates rise, the bond becomes less attractive to investors.* (MC: Bard should be saying that the **coupon** not yield is fixed)

*The risk of default is also high for HYG because the companies that issue high-yield bonds are considered to be more likely to default on their debt. This is because these companies are often in financial distress, and they may not be able to raise enough money to pay their bills.*

*Overall, HYG is a high-risk, high-reward investment. It is a good choice for investors who are looking for a way to **generate income in a rising interest rate environment**. However, it is not a good choice for investors who are looking for a safe investment.* (MC: Bard should elaborate further by explaining that in a rising interest rate environment, the economy is generally experiencing strong growth which in turn likely to support steady to rising cashflow for the firms)

2 basic points here:

1.  Fixed income securities are not boring. The returns can be very volatile especially Treasuries and High-Yield Bonds.
2.  Basic strategy is to study the trend in the economy data. In a weak economy buy TLT, and in a strong economy chose HYG.

An additional point is the LQD, the Investment Grade ETF has shown very steady returns, which means that the Sharpe ratio (which track the risk adjusted return) is very attractive. If one has no idea where the economy is going, LQD could be a good choice.

The price of TLT rallied from 135 in February 2020 to 170 in August 2020, an increase of 26% in just 6 months. This was a significant rally, and it is possible to make a lot of money by investing in TLT.

https://www.barchart.com/etfs-funds/quotes/TLT/interactive-chart

After the rally from February 2020 to August 2020, the price of TLT declined by 35% in the period ending in April 2022. This was a significant decline, and it is possible to lose a lot of money by investing in TLT.

# 10-year Treasury yield usually anticipated the end of Fed tightening

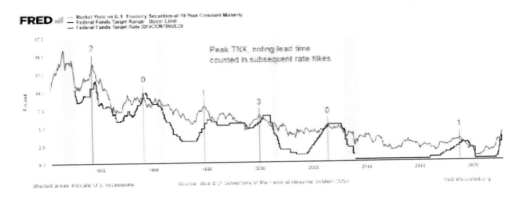

Prompt: 10-year Treasury yield usually anticipated the end of Fed tightening. True or false? Use data from FRED.

Perplexity:

Based on the data from FRED, the 10-Year Treasury yield is a measure of the yield on 10-year Treasury securities and is often used as a benchmark for long-term interest rates. The relationship between the 10-year Treasury yield and the end of Fed tightening is not always straightforward, but in general, the yield tends to anticipate the end of Fed tightening.

# Concept of The Business Cycle and Interest Rates

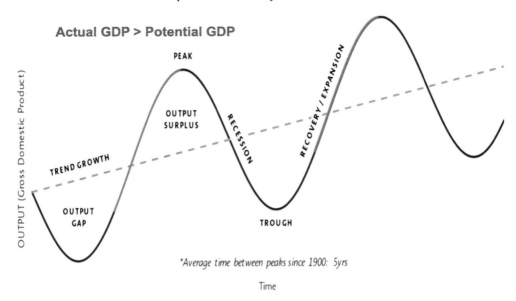

**Actual GDP > Potential GDP**

PEAK

OUTPUT (Gross Domestic Product)

OUTPUT
SURPLUS

RECESSION

RECOVERY / EXPANSION

TREND GROWTH

OUTPUT
GAP

TROUGH

*Average time between peaks since 1900: 5yrs*

Time

● Profitable to be LONG Interest Rates    ● Profitable to be SHORT Interest Rates

Source for chart: https://www.kesslercompanies.com/

Interest rates play a crucial role in predicting future economic activity. When the economy is growing above its potential GDP or trend growth rate, it tends to use up available resources, leading to inflationary pressures. As inflation rises, interest rates also increase. This rise in interest rates can make borrowing more expensive for businesses and individuals, resulting in a slowdown in economic growth and subsequently the interest rate declines.

Conversely, when economic activity slows down, interest rates tend to decline. Lower interest rates make borrowing cheaper, which encourages businesses to invest and expand, and consumers to borrow and spend more, boosting economic growth and leading to higher interest rates.

Interest rates also heavily influence the real estate market. Low interest rates make it more affordable for people to borrow money for home purchases, leading to increased demand and higher home prices. On the other hand, high interest rates make borrowing more expensive, leading to decreased demand and potentially lower home prices.

# Rare for High Quality Bonds to Have Two Straight Negative Years

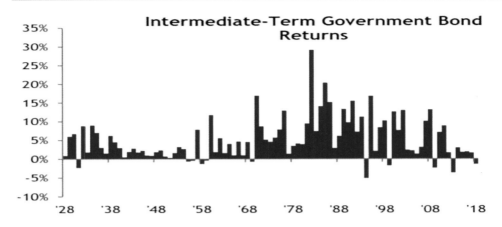

Data Source: Morningstar
Intermediate-term government bonds are represented by the IA SBBI US Intermediate-Term Government Bond Index: the index measures the performance of a single issue of outstanding US Treasury note with a maturity term of around 5.5 years. It is calculated by Morningstar and the raw data is from Wall Street Journal.

When a government bond fund experiences losses in year 1, it indicates that interest rates have increased. As a result, the prices of the bonds within the fund have declined, and this decline is more significant than the total coupon payments received during that period. If the negative return continues into year 2, it means that interest rates have continued to rise over the two-year period, surpassing the total coupon payments received throughout that time. Two consecutive years of rising interest rates generally means interest rates have risen enough to slow down the economy.

As we discussed earlier, higher interest rates have implications for borrowing costs. When interest rates are elevated, it becomes more expensive for businesses to borrow money, which can deter new business creation and hinder the expansion of existing businesses. As a consequence, more businesses may face contraction and be forced to lay off employees. The economy then slows down and interest rate declines which tend lead to a gain in bond prices.

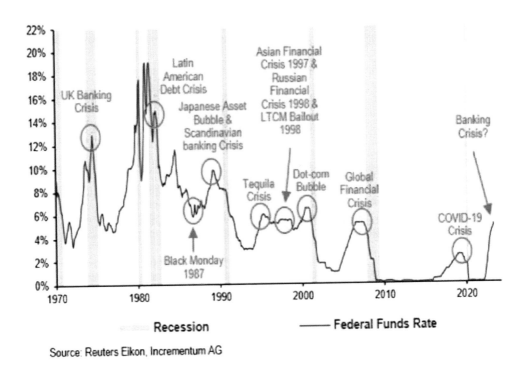

Source: Reuters Eikon, Incrementum AG

The chart shows that the Federal Reserve has a history of implementing overly restrictive monetary policies, which has led to economic crises. One reason for this is that the Fed often waits too long to respond to inflationary pressures. Inflation can persist for a while before the Fed raises interest rates, and this is often because the Fed wants to be sure that inflation is a serious problem before acting. However, by the time the Fed does act, inflation may have already gotten out of control.

Another consequence of the Fed's tightening measures is that it makes it more difficult for borrowers to refinance their maturing debt. Borrowers not only face higher interest rates, but they may also be subject to stricter lending conditions from banks. As the Fed continues to tighten monetary policy, banks become more hesitant to lend because they see an increased risk of a recession. This can become a self-fulfilling prophecy: if banks reduce lending because they are worried about a recession, their actions can actually help to cause a recession.

The Federal Reserve faces a risk of overtightening monetary policy because there can be a lag before the full effects of rate hikes are reflected in inflation. The Fed aims to see clear evidence that inflation is on a sustainable downward path closer to its target level before easing policy again. However, inflation often does not begin to ease significantly until after the economy has already slowed substantially. This lag creates potential for the Fed to keep rates high even after the tightening has started to reduce inflationary pressures, leading to unintended economic weakness.

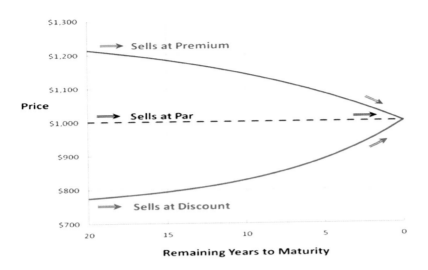

https://www.bogleheads.org/wiki/Bond_pricing

As a buy-and-hold investor, it is important to know that bond prices tend to gravitate towards their par value as they approach maturity. Par value is the face value of a bond, which is usually $1,000. This means that if you buy a bond and hold it until maturity, you are likely to get your money back.

Referring to the accompanying diagram, if an investor experiences a marked-to-market loss on their bond investment but has sufficient resources to avoid selling the bond and realizing the loss, they have the option to hold the position until maturity to recover from the losses and receive par.

If you initially purchased a bond at $1,000 and now observe that it is trading above $1,200, you are in a favorable position. You can choose to sell the bond and capture the profit, or you can opt to retain the investment. If you retain the investment, you are taking the risk that the price will pull to par and eventually return to $1,000, hence giving away what could have been a $200 profit.

**Chapter 4 Questions:**

1) Which asset exhibits the most price volatility?
a) Treasuries
b) Investment grade bonds
c) High yield bonds
d) Equities

Answer: d) Equities

Explanation: The reading identifies equities as having the highest volatility.

2) Based on the bell curve histogram, over what range did most annual returns on 30-year Treasuries fall?
a) -30% to -45%
b) 0% to 10%
c) 30% to 40%
d) Above 40%

Answer: b) 0% to 10%

Explanation: The histogram shows most returns between 0-10% annually.

3) During economic recoveries, junk bond performance tends to _____.
a) Lag investment grade bonds
b) Lead Treasuries
c) Underperform
d) Outperform

Answer: d) Outperform

Explanation: The reading states junk bonds tend to outperform in recoveries.

4) A key driver of Treasury yields is:
a) Corporate profits
b) Expected inflation
c) Trade deficits
d) Unemployment

Answer: b) Expected inflation

Explanation: The text identifies inflation expectations as a major Treasury yield factor.

5) A flattening yield curve often signals:

a) Economic growth
b) Low inflation
c) Tightening monetary policy
d) Economic slowdown

Answer: d) Economic slowdown

Explanation: The chapter associates a flattening curve with growth concerns.

6) HYG saw a sharp loss in 2008 MOST likely due to:
a) Rising inflation
b) Central bank policy
c) Equity market losses
d) Widening credit spreads

Answer: d) Widening credit spreads

Explanation: The reading attributes the HYG loss to high yield spread expansion.

7) Interest rate risk is _____ for longer maturity bonds.
a) Lower
b) Moderate
c) Exaggerated
d) Higher

Answer: d) Higher

Explanation: The text notes longer bonds have elevated interest rate sensitivity.

8) Which circumstance typically decreases Treasury yields?
a) Strong economic growth
b) High inflation
c) Rising commodity prices
d) Fed interest rate cuts

Answer: d) Fed interest rate cuts

Explanation: The chapter associates Fed rate cuts with declining Treasury yields.

9) Based on the reading, a bond selling above par will have a yield that is:
a) Negative
b) Less than its coupon
c) Equal to its coupon
d) Above its coupon

Answer: b) Less than its coupon

Explanation: The text states above-par bonds have yields below coupons.

10) Compared to other bonds, Treasuries are LEAST exposed to which risk?
a) Inflation risk
b) Interest rate risk
c) Liquidity risk
d) Default risk

Answer: d) Default risk

Explanation: The reading notes Treasuries have minimal default risk.

11) When are investors likely to favor long-term Treasuries?
a) Rising rate environment
b) High inflation
c) Economic stability
d) Tightening monetary policy

Answer: c) Economic stability

Explanation: The text associates stability with demand for longer Treasuries.

12) Based on the histogram, 30-year Treasury returns above 20% occurred approximately _____ of years.
a) 2%
b) 15%
c) 95%
d) 99%

Answer: b) 15%

Explanation: The histogram shows returns over 20% around 15% of the time.

13) High yield bonds are MOST susceptible to ___ risk.
a) Inflation
b) Liquidity
c) Prepayment
d) Default

Answer: d) Default

Explanation: The text identifies default risk as most relevant for high yield.

14) Compared to other bonds, TLT's returns are MORE sensitive to:
a) Inflation expectations
b) Corporate profits
c) Interest rate changes
d) Trade policy

Answer: c) Interest rate changes

Explanation: The reading emphasizes TLT's interest rate sensitivity.

15) During recessions, demand for high yield bonds tends to _____ relative to Treasuries.
a) Remain steady
b) Increase
c) Fluctuate randomly
d) Decrease

Answer: d) Decrease

Explanation: The text notes high yield bonds weaken versus Treasuries in recessions.

# Chapter 5 – Treasury Bonds and Notes – Duration as a Measure of Risk

**The Hidden Risk in Bonds**

Most people think of bonds as safe investments, but there is a hidden risk in bonds that many investors don't understand: interest rate risk.

Interest rate risk is the risk for a bond's price to decrease when interest rates rise. This is because the value of a bond is based on the present value of its future cash flows. When interest rates rise, the present value of those cash flows goes down, which means the price of the bond goes down.

The amount of interest rate risk in a bond is measured by its duration. Duration is a measure of how much the price of a bond will change if interest rates change.

The formula for calculating the percentage change in the price of a bond is:
Percentage change in price = - duration * (change in yield)

For example, if the duration of a bond is 5 years and the change in yield is 1%. Then, the percentage change in the price of the bond would be:
Percentage change in price = -5 * 1 = -5%

**TLT (20+ Year Treasuries) and SHY (1-3 Year Treasuries) Rate of Return**

In the image above, note how much more volatile TLT is, compared to SHY. TLT earned 33.92 percent in 2008 and then lost 21.80 percent in 2009. On the other hand, if you look at the rates of return for SHY, you will see that they were moderate in comparison.

**Prompt: What is the difference between TLT and SHY?**

Bard:

TLT and SHY are both exchange-traded funds (ETFs) that track the performance of U.S. Treasury bonds. However, they have different maturities and therefore different risk and return profiles. TLT (iShares 20+ Year Treasury Bond ETF) tracks the performance of the ICE U.S. Treasury 20+ Year Bond Index. This index includes Treasury bonds with maturities of 20 years or more. TLT has a long duration and is considered to be a risky investment.

SHY (iShares 1-3 Year Treasury Bond ETF) tracks the performance of the Barclays US 1-3 Year Treasury Bond Index. This index includes Treasury bonds with maturities of 1 to 3 years. SHY has a short duration and is considered to be a safe investment.

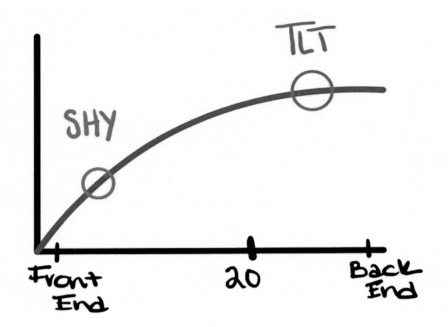

Source: Michelle Sanchez Aldana Gonzalez

Risk in the (Treasury) bond market is estimated using Duration

Percentage change in the price of bond
= - Duration X (Change in yield)

Note: The formula uses Modified Duration, not Macaulay Duration
Good to know if ....

## The Negative Sign in the Duration Formula

The negative sign in the duration formula simply reflects this inverse relationship between interest rates and bond prices. So, when you calculate the percentage change in the price of a bond, the negative sign in the duration formula ensures that the change in price is positive when interest rates decline and negative when interest rates rise.

## How is duration calculated?

Duration is calculated as the weighted average of the present value of all future cash flows, with the weights being the time to maturity of each cash flow. For example, a bond with a $100 face value that pays $5 in interest every year for 10 years and then matures for $100 has a duration of 5.7 years. This is because the present value of the first year's interest payment is $4.76, the present value of the second year's interest payment is $4.52, and so on. The time to maturity of each cash flow is weighted according to its present value, and the weighted average of these time to maturities is 5.7 years.

## What does it mean if a bond has a high duration?

A bond with a high duration means that the price of the bond is more sensitive to interest rate changes. For example, a bond with a duration of 10 years will lose more value if interest rates rise by 1% than a bond with a duration of 5 years.

## What does it mean if a bond has a low duration?

A bond with a low duration means that the price of the bond is less sensitive to interest rate changes. For example, a bond with a duration of 1 year will lose less value if interest rates rise by 1% than a bond with a duration of 10 years.

**How can investors use duration to manage their risk?**

Investors can use duration to manage their interest rate risk by choosing bonds with the right duration for their investment goals. For example, if an investor is concerned about interest rate risk, they might want to choose bonds with a shorter duration.

The duration of SHY (iShares 1-3 Year Treasury Bond ETF) is about 1.8 years.

**But what if you expect interest rates to fall?**

In this case, you might want to consider buying bonds with longer durations. This is because the price of bonds with longer durations will go up when interest rates fall.

For example, let's say that you buy a bond with a duration of 10 years, and interest rates fall by 1%. The price of your bond will go up by about 10%.

As an alternative to bonds with 10 years duration, investors could take on even more duration risk by buying the TLT which has a duration of 17-18 years.

**The Difference Between Modified Duration and Macaulay Duration**

Modified duration and Macaulay duration are two measures of a bond's interest rate sensitivity. They are both calculated as the weighted average of the time to maturity of a bond's cash flows, but the weights are different.

In the modified duration formula, the weights are the present values of the cash flows. This means that the modified duration takes into account the time value of money. The Macaulay duration formula, on the other hand, uses the undiscounted cash flows.

This difference in the weights means that modified duration is a more accurate measure of a bond's interest rate sensitivity than Macaulay duration. However, modified duration is also more complex to calculate.

In the industry, either modified duration or Macaulay duration is used to estimate the percentage change in price of a bond. However, modified duration is generally preferred because it is more accurate.

## Which One Should You Use?

If you are writing an academic paper, you should use modified duration because it is the more accurate measure of interest rate sensitivity. However, if you are just trying to estimate the percentage change in price of a bond, either modified duration or Macaulay duration will be fine.

## 1. Duration Depends on Maturity

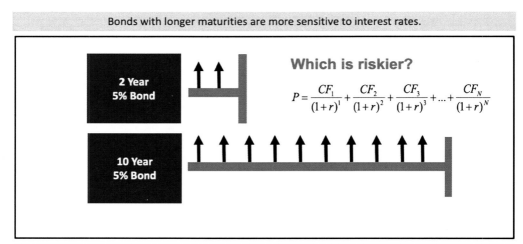

Bonds with longer maturities are more sensitive to interest rates.

**Which is riskier?**

$$P = \frac{CF_1}{(1+r)^1} + \frac{CF_2}{(1+r)^2} + \frac{CF_3}{(1+r)^3} + ... + \frac{CF_N}{(1+r)^N}$$

| Capital Gain/Loss per $10,000 Invested | | |
|---|---|---|
| **_Market Yield Change:_** | **- 1.00%** | **+ 1.00%** |
| 2 Year | +$197 | -$197 |
| 5 Year | +$478 | -$478 |
| 10 Year | +$839 | -$839 |

*Note: Price changes are approximate, meant for purpose of illustration.*

*Source: Bloomberg as of 10/25/2010.*

**Duration depends on maturity.**

The longer the maturity of a bond, the higher its duration. This is because bonds with longer maturities have more cash flows that are further out in the future. The illustration above shows a 2-year 5% bond and a 10-year 5% bond. As you can see in the table of Capital Gain/Loss, the 10-year Treasury bond is riskier. For a 1.00% drop-in interest rate, the 2-year bond makes a return of $197, while the 10-year treasury bond makes a return of $839. On the other hand, when interest rates increase by 1%, the 2-year bond has a loss of $197 and the 10-year treasury bond has a loss of $839. This shows how when the interest rate drops, the price goes up and vice versa, as well as illustrates how bonds with a longer maturity are riskier.

## Why does duration depend on maturity?

The reason why duration depends on maturity is because bonds with longer maturities have more cash flows that are further out in the future.

## What does this mean for investors?

For investors, this means that they need to be aware of the risk associated with bonds with longer maturities. If interest rates rise, then the price of these bonds will fall, which could lead to losses for investors.

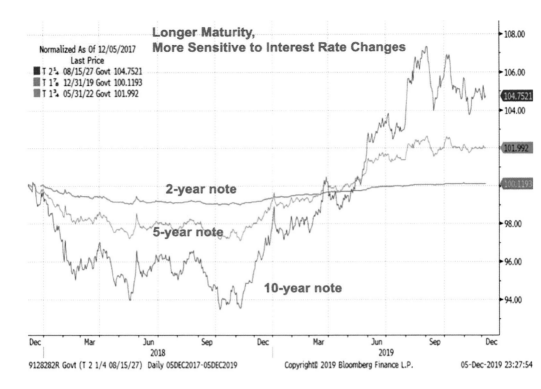

Bonds with longer maturities are more sensitive to interest rate changes.

The chart shows three different bonds, all indexed to start at 100, over the same period of time. You can see how the 10-year bond is more sensitive to interest rate changes, given that it drops to 94 and then increases to 107, while the 2-year note practically stays at the same level, trading not far away from the 100 mark. This is because the 10-year bond has a longer maturity than the 2-year note.

Note that these bonds have similar coupon rates and hence do not affect the duration too much.

## 2. Duration Depends on Coupon

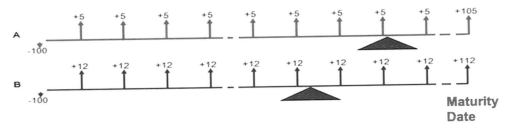

- Which is riskier? A or B?
- How long, in years, it takes for the price of a bond to be repaid by its internal cash flow?
- Time Weighted Cash Flow. Macaulay Duration

---

**Higher coupons = Lower duration**

---

Maturity and coupon rate are two factors that affect a bond's duration. The longer the maturity of a bond, the longer its duration. The higher the coupon rate of a bond, the shorter its duration.

In the illustration above, Bond A has a 5% coupon and Bond B has a 12% coupon; both with the same maturity date. This means that Bond A pays out $5 in interest every year, while Bond B pays out $12 in interest every year.

Since Bond B pays out more interest, it will take less time for Bond B to repay its price through its internal cash flows. This means that Bond B has a shorter duration than Bond A. Hence, A is riskier.

A higher coupon rate means a lower duration. This is because a higher coupon rate means that more of the bond's price is paid out in interest payments, which are received sooner. Macaulay duration is a measure of a bond's price sensitivity to interest rate changes. It is calculated as the weighted average of the time to maturity of all future cash flows, with the weights being the present value of each cash flow.

For example, consider a bond with a coupon rate of 5% and a maturity of 10 years. The bond pays interest semiannually, so it has 20 coupon payments. The present value of each coupon payment is calculated using a discount rate of 6%. The Macaulay duration of this bond is 6.7 years.

This means that, on average, it will take 6.7 years for the price of this bond to be repaid by its internal cash flows. This is because the present value of the early coupon payments is weighted more heavily in the Macaulay duration calculation than the present value of the later coupon payments.

Investors who are concerned about interest rate risk should invest in bonds with shorter Macaulay durations.

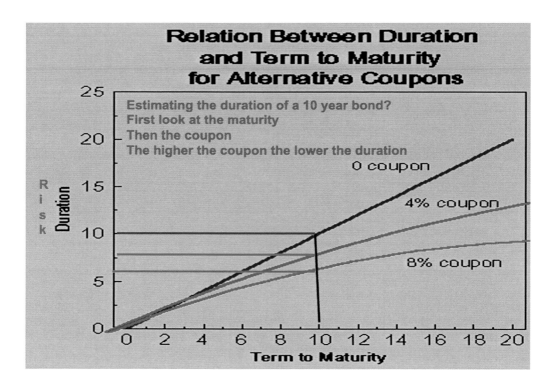

Source: http://people.duke.edu/~charvey/Classes/ba350_1997/bondval/bondval.htm

The graph above shows the relationship between the coupon rate and the duration for 10-year bonds. As you can see, a 10-year bond with a 0% coupon has a duration of 10 years. The time-weighted cashflow is the same as the one and only final payment at the end of the maturity date.

When you compare it with a 10-year bond with a 4% coupon, you can see that the duration drops to 8 years. When you compare that to a 10-year bond with an 8% coupon, it drops again to 6 years. This is because the higher the coupon rate, the interest payments are received sooner, which means that the bond is less sensitive to interest rate changes.

**=DURATION (settlement, maturity, coupon, yld, freq, [basis])**

# Excel DURATION Function

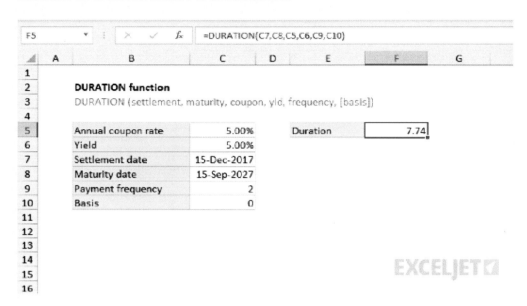

https://exceljet.net/excel-functions/excel-duration-function

https://www.educba.com/convexity-formula/

**Prompt: What is the excel formula for duration?**

Bard:

=DURATION(settlement,maturity,coupon,yld,frequency,basis)

Here is a breakdown of the arguments:

Settlement: The date on which the bond was purchased or settled.

Maturity: The date on which the bond matures.

Coupon: The annual coupon rate of the bond.

Yield : The annual yield of the bond.

Frequency: The number of coupon payments per year.

Basis: The day count basis to be used for calculations.

The default value for basis is 0 or omitted, which uses the US (NASD) 30/360 day count convention.

For example, to calculate the duration of a bond with a settlement date of 2/1/2023, maturity date of 2/1/2028, coupon rate of 5%, yield of 4%, frequency of semiannual, and US (NASD) 30/360 day count basis, you would use the following formula:

=DURATION(2/1/2023,2/1/2028,5%,4%,2,0)

The result would be 7.2 years.

It is important to note that the duration of a bond is a measure of its price sensitivity to interest rate changes. It does not measure the total return of a bond. The total return of a bond is affected by several factors, including interest rate changes, coupon payments, and reinvestment rates.

Number of Years to Maturity:

```
10
```

Yield or Market Rate (%):

```
1
```

Bond Face Value:

```
1000
```

Annual Coupon Rate (%):

```
1
```

○ Annually
⦿ Semiannually
○ Quarterly
○ Monthly

Calculate Bond Duration

Macaulay Duration: 9.541

Modified Duration: 9.494

Source: **https://exploringfinance.com/bond-duration-calculator/**

There are a number of websites that can help you calculate the duration of a bond, such as www.exploringfinance.com. To use this website, simply enter the following information:

Number of years to maturity: This is the number of years until the bond matures.

Yield or market rate (%): This is the current yield or market rate for similar bonds.

Bond face value: This is the amount of money that will be paid to the bondholder when the bond matures.

Annual coupon rate (%): This is the percentage of the bond face value that will be paid to the bondholder as interest each year.

Once you have entered this information, the website will calculate the Macaulay duration and the modified duration of the bond. The Macaulay duration is a measure of how much the price of the bond will change in response to a change in interest rates. The modified duration is a more accurate measure of price sensitivity to interest rates, but it is only applicable to bonds that pay periodic interest payments.

In the example above, the Macaulay duration is 9.541 and the modified duration is 9.494. This means that the price of the bond will change by approximately 9.5% if interest rates change by 1%.

It is important to note that the duration of a bond is not a static number. It will change over time as interest rates change and as the bond gets closer to maturity.

Another helpful website is:

https://www.money-education.com/resources/calculators/duration-calculation

## 10-Year Treasury Yield Box and Whiskers Chart

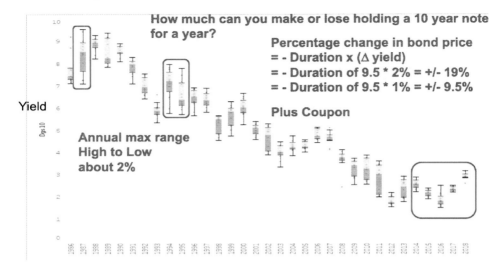

The image above shows a box and whiskers chart of a 10-year Treasury Yield. The box shows the middle 50% of the data, the whiskers show the data that is within 1.5 times the interquartile range of the middle 50%, and the outliers are the data that is more than 1.5 times the interquartile range away from the middle 50%.

We can use this chart to estimate the maximum range of a 10-year Treasury Yield. The maximum range is the difference between the highest and lowest values in the data. In this case, the maximum range is 2%. This means that the 10-year Treasury Yield could theoretically change by up to 2% in a year.

However, it is important to note that the maximum range is just an estimate. The actual change in the 10-year Treasury Yield could be more or less than 2%. For example, if there is a major economic event, such as a surge in inflation or a financial crisis, the 10-year Treasury Yield could change by more than 2%.

To calculate the potential loss or gain of a 10-year Treasury Yield, we can use the following formula:

Potential loss or gain = -Duration * (Change in Yield)

In this formula, duration is the measure of how much the price of a bond will change in response to a change in interest rates and change in yield is the percentage change in the yield of a bond. For example, if a 10-year Treasury Yield has a duration of 9.5 and the yield changes by 2%, the potential loss or gain would be -/+19%.

If an investor feels that the more recent ranges of about 1% is more likely to be repeated in the near future, then given the same duration of 9.5 and the yield changes by 1%, the estimated potential loss or gain would be -/+9.5%.

# Impact of a 1% fall in interest rates

Assumes a parallel shift in the yield curve

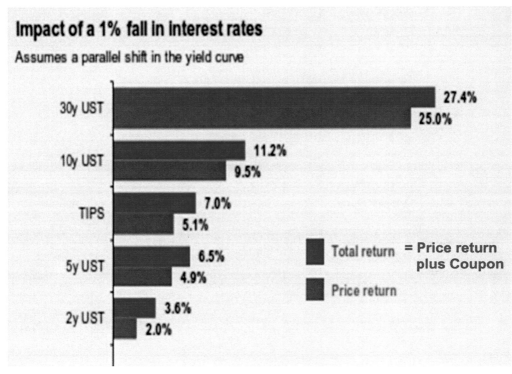

Source: JP Morgan

Every now and then, you may see news reports from companies such as JPMorgan Chase & Co. that discuss the impact of a 1% fall in interest rates. However, the total return of a bond is not just the price return. The total return also includes the coupon payments that the bondholder receives.

The coupon payment is the amount of interest that the bondholder receives each year. For a 10-year UST, the coupon payment could be 2% of the bond's face value. So, if a 10-year UST has a face value of $1,000 and the coupon rate is 2%, the bondholder will receive $20 in interest payments each year.

The total return of a bond is calculated using the following formula:

Total return = Price return + Coupon payments

For example, if a 10-year UST has a duration of 9.5, the yield falls by 1%, and the coupon rate is 2%, the total return would be 11.2%.

Note that the estimated change in price for a 30-year Treasury bond is 25% for every 1% change in interest rate. This suggests that the duration of the bond is 25 years.

# US Treasury Securities Valuation Calculator

A tool for estimating the effect of interest rate fluctuations on market price for Treasury security holdings

Source: https://www.ustreasuryyieldcurve.com/

The website is not an official website of the U.S. Treasury, but it provides a tool that allows you to explore the U.S. Treasury yield curve.

You can begin with a starting level of market interest rate and the corresponding market price, and the tool will map out where prices are likely to be when interest rates change.

The line that the tool generates is not a straight line, but rather it is convex. This means that the change in price is not proportional to the change in interest rate. For example, if interest rates increase by 1%, the price may decrease by less than 1%.

**Portfolio Duration**

□ Example:

| Bond | Market Value | Weight | Duration |
|------|-------------|--------|----------|
| A | $10 million | 0.10 | 4 |
| B | $40 million | 0.40 | 7 |
| C | $30 million | 0.30 | 6 |
| D | $20 million | 0.20 | 2 |

□ Portfolio duration is: $0.10 \cdot 4 + 0.40 \cdot 7 + 0.30 \cdot 6 + 0.20 \cdot 2 = 5.40$

□ If all the yields affecting the four bonds change by 100 bps, the value of the portfolio will change by about 5.4%.

Source: Cengage

The riskiness of a bond portfolio can be estimated by looking at its weighted average duration. This is the average duration of the bonds in the portfolio, weighted by their market values.

For example, let's say we have a portfolio of four bonds, A, B, C, and D, with a total market value of $100 million. The weights of each bond are calculated by dividing each individual market value by 100 million.

Bond A has a market value of $10 million, so its weight is 0.10.
Bond B has a market value of $40 million, so its weight is 0.40.
Bond C has a market value of $30 million, so its weight is 0.30.
Bond D has a market value of $20 million, so its weight is 0.20.

The durations of the bonds are 4 years, 7 years, 6 years, and 2 years, respectively. To calculate the portfolio duration, we multiply the weights of each bond by its duration and then add the results.

Portfolio duration = 0.10 * 4 + 0.40 * 7 + 0.30 * 6 + 0.20 * 2 = 5.40 years

This means that for every one percent movement in interest rates, the portfolio will change in value by 5.4%.

If we expect interest rates to rise, we should lower the duration of our portfolio. This can be done by selling some of the longer-term bonds in the portfolio and buying more short-term bonds.

By lowering the duration of the portfolio, we can reduce the risk of the portfolio losing value if interest rates rise. However, it is important to note that lowering the duration of the portfolio may also reduce the potential returns of the portfolio.

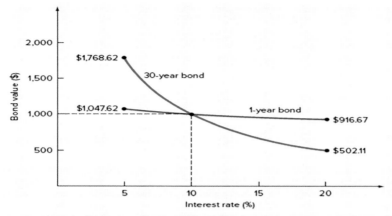

Value of a Bond with a 10 Percent Coupon Rate for Different Interest Rates and Maturities

|  | Time to Maturity | |
| Interest Rate | 1 Year | 30 Years |
| --- | --- | --- |
| 5% | $1,047.62 | $1,768.62 |
| 10 | 1,000.00 | 1,000.00 |
| 15 | 956.52 | 671.70 |
| 20 | 916.67 | 502.11 |

Source: Cengage

## The Limitations of Duration

Duration does not consider the convexity of a bond. Convexity is a measure of the curvature of the bond's price-yield curve. Bonds with positive convexity will experience a larger price increase than what duration would predict when interest rates fall but will experience a smaller price decrease than what duration would predict when interest rates rise.

Convexity is often ignored in bond pricing because it is often small and does not have a significant impact on the estimated percentage change in price when we expect small changes in interest rates. However, if interest rates are expected to change by a large amount, then the convexity term can become important.

The full formula for estimating the percentage change in the price of a bond when interest rates change is:

Percentage change in price = -duration * (change in yield) + convexity * (change in yield)^2

**Chapter 5 Questions:**

1. Which of the following statements about duration is true?
A) Duration measures the total return of a bond.
B) Duration measures the interest rate sensitivity of a bond.
C) Bonds with longer durations are less sensitive to interest rate changes.
D) Duration increases as the coupon rate increases.

Explanation: B is correct. Duration measures the interest rate sensitivity of a bond, not the total return. Bonds with longer durations are more sensitive to interest rate changes. Duration decreases as the coupon rate increases.

2. If a bond has a duration of 8 years, what will happen to the bond's price if interest rates increase by 2%?
A) The price will increase by 16%
B) The price will decrease by 16%
C) The price will increase by 8%
D) The price will decrease by 8%

Explanation: B is correct. Using the duration formula: % change in price = -duration * change in yield = -8 * 2% = -16%. So the price will decrease by 16%.

3. Which bond has the longer duration?
A) A 10-year bond with a 12% coupon
B) A 10-year bond with a 5% coupon
C) A 5-year bond with a 12% coupon
D) A 5-year bond with a 5% coupon

Explanation: B is correct. Given the same maturity, a lower coupon bond will have a longer duration because less of the cash flows are received earlier.

4. If a bond portfolio has a weighted average duration of 7 years, what will happen to the portfolio if interest rates increase by 1%?
A) The portfolio value will increase by 7%
B) The portfolio value will decrease by 7%
C) The portfolio value will not change
D) The portfolio value will increase by 14%

Explanation: B is correct. Using the portfolio duration formula, the portfolio value will decrease by 7% (duration * change in yield = 7 * 1% = 7%).

5. Which of the following affects the duration of a bond?
A) The frequency of coupon payment
B) The time to maturity

C) The credit rating
D) The face value

Explanation: B is correct. Frequency of coupon payment and credit rating and face value do not affect duration.

6. If you expect interest rates to rise, which bonds should you invest in to minimize interest rate risk?
A) Long-term zero coupon bonds
B) Long-term bonds with high coupons
C) Short-term bonds with low coupons
D) Short-term bonds with high coupons

Explanation: D is correct. To minimize interest rate risk when rates are expected to rise, invest in short-term bonds with high coupons, which have the shortest durations.

7. What does a bond's convexity measure?
A) The bond's interest rate sensitivity
B) The bond's price volatility
C) The curvature of the bond's price-yield curve
D) The total return of the bond

Explanation: C is correct. Convexity measures the curvature or shape of the bond's price-yield curve.

8. If a bond's duration is 10 and yield changes by 1%, what is the estimated price change?
A) 10%
B) -10%
C) 20%
D) -20%

Explanation: B is correct. Using the duration formula: % change in price = -duration * change in yield = -10 * 1% = -10%

9. Which has a higher interest rate risk - TLT or SHY?
A) TLT
B) SHY
C) They have equal interest rate risk
D) It cannot be determined

Explanation: A is correct. TLT tracks long-term Treasuries so it has a higher duration and more interest rate risk. SHY tracks short-term Treasuries.

10. What does a long duration bond indicate?
A) The bond matures soon
B) The bond has high interest rate sensitivity
C) The bond has high credit risk
D) The bond has a high coupon rate

Explanation: B is correct. Long duration indicates high interest rate sensitivity.

11. What is the relationship between maturity and duration?
A) They are inversely related
B) They are directly related
C) There is no relationship
D) The relationship depends on the coupon rate

Explanation: B is correct. Longer maturity leads to higher duration, all else equal.

12. What is the formula for calculating duration?
A) Duration = (Maturity * Coupon) / Yield
B) Duration = Maturity - Coupon
C) Duration = Maturity + Coupon
D) Duration = (Maturity * Yield) / Coupon
E) None of the above

Explanation: E is correct. There is no simple formula. Duration depends on the timing of cash flows which depends on maturity, coupon rate and yield.

13. How can an investor reduce interest rate risk?
A) Invest in long-term zero coupon bonds
B) Shorten the portfolio duration
C) Lengthen the portfolio duration
D) Invest in bonds with high credit risk

Explanation: B is correct. Shortening the portfolio duration by investing in shorter-term bonds reduces interest rate risk.

# Chapter 6 – Treasury Notes and Bonds – Zero Coupon Bonds

**Prompt: What is a zero-coupon bond?**

Bard:
A zero-coupon bond is a debt instrument that does not pay interest until maturity. Instead, investors buy the bond at a deep discount from its face value, which is the amount the investor will receive when the bond matures. The difference between the purchase price of the bond and the face value is the investor's return.

Here are some of the advantages of zero-coupon bonds:

Guaranteed return: The investor knows exactly how much they will earn from the bond, as the return is fixed at the time of purchase.

Long maturities: Zero-coupon bonds are often issued with long maturities, which can appeal to investors who are looking for a long-term investment.

Here are some of the disadvantages of zero-coupon bonds:

No interest payments: Zero-coupon bonds do not pay interest until maturity, so investors do not receive any income until the bond matures.

Price volatility: The price of a zero-coupon bond is more volatile than the price of a regular bond, as it is more sensitive to changes in interest rates.

Long-term risk: Zero-coupon bonds are a long-term investment, so investors should be prepared for the possibility of losses if interest rates rise significantly before the bond matures.

**Matching strategy with a zero-coupon bond**

**a) Pension fund with a defined liability**

$$P = \frac{0}{(1+r)^1} + \frac{0}{(1+r)^2} + \frac{0}{(1+r)^3} + ... + \frac{100}{(1+r)^N}$$

r    = RR + IP + MP

RR = the real rate of interest
IP  = the inflation premium
MP = the maturity premium

When CF1 to CF(N-1) =0
and CF$_N$ = 100 ?

Zero coupon bond

Source: Fabozzi Chapter 9

**Prompt: Why would a pension fund with a defined liability, say to pay $10 million in 10 years time would buy a 10-year zero coupon?**

Bard:

A pension fund with a defined liability, such as a promise to pay $10 million in 10 years, might buy a 10-year zero-coupon bond for a few reasons.

**To match the maturity of the liability.** A 10-year zero-coupon bond will mature when the liability is due. If interest rates rise, the value of the bond will fall, but since the pension fund is holding to maturity, the pull to par will bring the value of the bond up and reduce the loss over time.

**To lock in a fixed interest rate.** The interest rate on a zero-coupon bond is fixed at zero when the bond is issued, so the pension fund knows exactly how much money it will receive over the

10 years. Without any coupon payments, this can help to protect the pension fund from reinvestment risk.

**To earn a higher yield than a traditional bond**. Because zero-coupon bonds are not paying interest until maturity, they typically offer a higher yield than traditional bonds.

**To pay a lower upfront cost.** The present value (PV) or price of the bond would be lower because there are no coupon payments in the future.

**Liquidity risk**. Zero-coupon bonds are not as liquid as traditional bonds, which means that they may be more difficult to sell if the pension fund needs to raise cash or the assumptions for paying its liabilities have changed materially.

**Matching strategy with a zero-coupon bond**

**b) Create principal guaranteed products**

## Enter Your Bond Information

| | |
|---|---|
| Face value at maturity | 100000 |
| Interest rate (APR %) | 3 |
| Years to maturity | 10 |
| Bond purchase price | $74,247.04 |
| Nominal return | $25,752.96 |

**Invest in stocks options/warrants**

Source: https://calculator.me/savings/**zero-coupon-bonds.php**

Suppose you have $100,000 now and you won't require the funds for the next 10 years. You do not wish to lose any money yet wish to be invested in the stock market. Here is what you can do:

Buy a $100,000 zero-coupon 10-year Treasury bond. A zero-coupon bond is a bond that does not pay interest until it matures. However, the bond will be worth $100,000 when it matures, regardless of what happens to interest rates or the stock market in the meantime.

Invest the remaining $25,753 in the stock market directly or buy a 10-year warrant. A warrant is a type of derivative that gives you the right but not obligated to buy a certain number of shares of stock at a fixed price on or before a certain date. This means that you can limit your downside risk in the stock market by only investing the amount of money that you are willing to lose.

Even if you lose the entire $25,753 invested in the stock market, you will still end up with $100,000 when the zero-coupon bond matures in 10 years. This strategy can help you to achieve your investment goals of preserving your capital and gaining exposure to the stock market without taking on too much risk.

## Chapter 6 – Questions: Zero Coupon Bond

1. Which of the following is a disadvantage of zero-coupon bonds?
A) Lack of liquidity
B) Price volatility
C) Long maturities
D) Guaranteed return

Answer: B
Explanation: Zero-coupon bonds have higher price volatility compared to coupon bonds because they are more sensitive to interest rate changes. For bond with the same maturity, the zero coupon has the longest duration.

2. If a pension fund needs to pay out $10 million in 10 years, what duration zero-coupon bond could it buy?
A) 5-year zero coupon
B) 10-year zero coupon
C) 15-year zero coupon
D) 20-year zero coupon

Answer: B
Explanation: A 10-year zero-coupon bond would match the 10-year liability of the pension fund.

3. How can an investor limit downside risk when investing in stocks using zero-coupon bonds?
A) Invest in mutual funds
B) Use options contracts
C) Buy zero-coupon bonds as principal protection
D) Diversify across asset classes

Answer: C
Explanation: Zero-coupon bonds provide principal protection, so buying them allows investors to limit downside risk when investing in stocks.

4. What happens to the yield of a zero-coupon bond over its life?
A) The yield increases each year
B) The yield decreases each year
C) The yield remains unchanged
D) The yield fluctuates each year

Answer: D
Explanation: The yield of a zero-coupon bond fluctuates depending on market supply and demand for such bond. It is the coupon (in this case, it is zero) that remains unchanged

5. Which has greater price sensitivity to interest rates - a 10-year zero coupon bond or a 10-year coupon bond?
A) 10-year zero coupon bond
B) 10-year coupon bond
C) They have equal sensitivity
D) It depends on the coupon rate

Answer: A
Explanation: A zero-coupon bond has greater interest rate sensitivity than a coupon bond of the same maturity.

6. Which of the following is an advantage of zero-coupon bonds?
A) Regular interest payments
B) Guaranteed return
C) Short maturities
D) High liquidity

Explanation: B is correct. Zero-coupon bonds provide a guaranteed return since the yield is fixed at purchase.

7. If interest rates rise after an investor purchases a zero-coupon bond, what will happen to the bond's price?
A) The price will increase
B) The price will decrease
C) The price will remain unchanged
D) The impact depends on the maturity

Explanation: B is correct. Zero-coupon bond prices will decline.

8. How can a pension fund benefit from buying a zero-coupon bond to fund a future liability?
A) The zero-coupon bond provides regular income
B) It locks in the yield and matches the maturity
C) Zero-coupon bonds have high liquidity
D) Zero-coupons have very long maturities

Explanation: B is correct. Zero-coupons allow pension funds to lock in the yield and match the maturity to their future liabilities.

# Chapter 7 – Treasury Inflation-Protected Securities – TIPS

**Prompt: What is Treasury Inflation-Protected Securities?**

Claude:
Treasury Inflation-Protected Securities (TIPS) are a type of Treasury bond designed to provide protection against inflation.

Key features of TIPS:

TIPS principal adjusts with inflation: The par value rises with the Consumer Price Index to maintain purchasing power. This adjusts the principal value to track inflation.

Pays a fixed interest rate: The coupon rate is set at time of issuance and paid semiannually. The rate applies to the inflation-adjusted principal.

Maturities range from 5 to 30 years: Investors can choose duration based on interest rate and inflation outlook.

Deflation floor on par value: Principal will not adjust below the original par value in case of deflation.

Sold at auction by the Treasury: Issues new TIPS on a regular schedule via competitive auction bidding.

Trades on the secondary market: Existing TIPS can be bought/sold between investors before maturity.

Lower yields than nominal Treasuries: TIPS pay lower nominal yields to compensate for the inflation protection.

**Treasury bonds**
- r = real rates + inflation premium + maturity premium

**TIPS**
- r = real rates + maturity premium

The inflation indexed bonds only have a two lego blocks compared to the three lego blocks before. In this case, the coupon rate is the real rate, the inflation adjusted rate, which is determined via auction. The price of the bond goes up when yield declines. Yield of TIPS = real rates + maturity premium. The price of TIPs can decline when real rates go up when inflation goes up. So, how is the total return affected by price change and coupon payment?

Here is the total return dynamics for TIPS:

**The TIPS yield has two components:**

Real interest rate
Maturity premium

If inflation rises, it will likely push up real interest rates since the Fed raises rates to contain inflation. Higher real rates mean higher TIPS yields, which causes TIPS prices to decline.

However, the total return for a TIPS holder has two elements:

Price return: Capital gain/loss from bond price changes
Income return: Interest payments received.

If TIPS prices decline due to higher real rates, it creates a negative price return. But the income return is based on the coupon rate.

As inflation rises, the coupon payments also increase since they are adjusted for inflation. So the higher coupon payment helps offset some of the price decline.

In total return terms, the income return from higher inflation-adjusted coupon payments helps cushion the negative price return from the increase in real rates. The total return would depend on the relative magnitude of the two effects. So, while higher inflation can hurt TIPS prices due to increased real rates, the inflation protection on the interest payments is a mitigating factor for total returns.

**TIPS**

- Coupon rate (real rate) is determined via auction.
- Inflation index is CPI-U.
- Inflation adjusted principal, adjusted semi-annually.
- Interest paid semi-annually = ½ coupon rate * inflation adjusted principal.
- If de/disinflation results in principle at maturity < 100, payment is par.

Tips are also known as inflation-indexed bonds or linkers.  The principal of an inflation-indexed bond is adjusted semi-annually based on a specified inflation index, such as the Consumer Price Index (CPI). This means that if inflation rises, the principal of the bond will increase, and investors will receive higher interest payments. Conversely, if inflation falls, the principal of the bond will decrease, and investors will receive lower interest payments.

The coupon rate of an inflation-indexed bond is the real rate of interest, which is determined via auction. The real rate of interest is the rate of interest that is earned after inflation has been considered.

The interest payments on an inflation-indexed bond are paid semi-annually. The amount of interest paid is calculated by multiplying the coupon rate by the inflation-adjusted principal. For example, if the coupon rate is 2% and the inflation-adjusted principal is $103,000, then the interest payment will be $2,060/2 which is $1,030 for that 6-month period.

If there is a de/disinflation, which means that inflation falls, the principal at maturity may be less than $100,000. In this case, the bondholder will still receive the face value of the bond, which is $100,000.

Inflation-indexed bonds are a good investment for investors who are concerned about inflation. They can help to protect investors' purchasing power and ensure that they receive a real return on their investment.

## Treasury Yields

| NAME | COUPON | PRICE | YIELD |
|---|---|---|---|
| GT2:GOV 2 Year | 3.25 | 99.66 | 3.43% |
| GT5:GOV 5 Year | 3.13 | 98.94 | 3.36% |
| GT10:GOV 10 Year | 2.75 | 95.67 | 3.26% |
| GT30:GOV 30 Year | 3.00 | 92.33 | 3.41% |

10 yr Treasury yield = 3.20%
10 yr TIPS yield     = 0.81%
Breakeven inflation
BEI                  = 2.39%

If actual inflation > BEI,
TIPS outperforms Treasury
bonds

## Treasury Inflation Protected Securities (TIPS)

| NAME | COUPON | PRICE | YIELD |
|---|---|---|---|
| GTII5:GOV 5 Year | 0.13 | 96.78 | 0.84% |
| GTII10:GOV 10 Year | 0.63 | 98.25 | 0.81% |

Source: https://www.bloomberg.com/markets/rates-bonds/government-bonds/usS, **Sep 7, 2022**

The break-even inflation (BEI) is the inflation rate at which a Treasury Inflation-Protected Security (TIPS) will have the same yield as a regular Treasury bond. In this case, the BEI is 2.39%. This means that if inflation is greater than 2.39%, TIPS will outperform regular Treasury bonds.

For example, if inflation turns out to be 4%, then a TIPS would provide a return of 4% + 0.81% = 4.81%. This is higher than the 3.26% yield from a regular Treasury bond. Conversely, if inflation turns out to be only 2%, then TIPS with a total return of 2.81% would underperform regular Treasury bonds.

Here is a table that summarizes the different scenarios:

| Inflation | TIPS return | Treasury bond return |
|---|---|---|
| 4% | 4.81% | 3.26% |
| 2% | 2.81% | 3.26% |
| 0% | 0.81% | 3.26% |

As you can see, TIPS will outperform regular Treasury bonds if inflation is greater than the BEI. However, TIPS will underperform regular Treasury bonds if inflation is less than or equal to the BEI.

## Chapter 7 Questions: TIPS

1. How does the principal value of TIPS change with inflation?
A) It decreases with inflation
B) It increases with inflation
C) It is unaffected by inflation
D) It has an inverse relationship

Explanation: B is correct. The par value of TIPS increases with inflation to maintain purchasing power.

2. Which TIPS return component typically increases when inflation rises?
A) Coupon payment
B) Price return
C) Maturity premium
D) Real interest rate

Explanation: A is correct. TIPS coupon payments increase with inflation since they are adjusted for changes in CPI.

3. How do TIPS help protect investors against inflation?
A) By paying a high fixed coupon rate
B) By adjusting the principal value for inflation
C) By having very long maturities
D) By being backed by the U.S. Treasury

Answer: B
Explanation: TIPS protect against inflation by adjusting their principal value based on changes in the CPI inflation index.

4. What is the coupon rate of TIPS based on?
A) Face value of the bond
B) Inflation-adjusted principal
C) Current Consumer Price Index
D) Real interest rate

Answer: D
Explanation: The TIPS coupon rate represents the real interest rate and does not change with inflation.

5. If actual inflation turns out higher than breakeven inflation, which bond will perform better?
A) TIPS

B) Treasury bonds
C) They will perform the same
D) Corporate bonds

Answer: A
Explanation: If actual inflation exceeds breakeven inflation, TIPS will outperform regular Treasury bonds.

# Chapter 8 – Corporate Bonds

Corporate bonds are a type of debt security issued by companies to raise capital. They are a form of borrowing for companies and are typically used to finance operations, expansion, or acquisitions. When investors purchase corporate bonds, they are essentially lending money to the issuing company in exchange for regular interest payments and the return of the principal amount at maturity.

For example, let's say that you are an investor who is interested in purchasing corporate bonds. You would want to understand the company's total debt before you make an investment. You could do this by looking at the company's balance sheet, which is a financial statement that shows the company's assets, liabilities, and equity. The total debt on the balance sheet would include all the company's corporate bonds, as well as any other forms of debt that the company has.

Understanding a company's total debt is crucial for assessing its financial stability and creditworthiness. If a company has a lot of debt, it may be more likely to default on its payments. This could have a negative impact on the company's stock price and its ability to raise capital in the future.

By analyzing the trend in total liabilities, investors and analysts can gain insights into the company's borrowing activities and its ability to manage its debt load. For example, if a company's total liabilities are increasing at a rapid pace, it could be a sign that the company is struggling to manage its debt load. This could be a red flag for investors, who may want to avoid investing in the company's bonds.

In addition to analyzing the trend in total liabilities, investors and analysts should also analyze the trend in liabilities vs assets. This ratio, known as the debt-to-equity ratio, can provide insights into the company's financial leverage. A high debt-to-equity ratio means that the company is using a lot of debt to finance its operations. This can be a red flag for investors, as it could mean that the company is more likely to default on its payments.

Another important factor to consider is the trend in cashflow. Cashflow is the amount of money that a company generates from its operations. A positive cashflow indicates that the company is generating enough money to cover its expenses and make its debt payments. A negative cashflow, on the other hand, could be a sign that the company is struggling to generate enough money to meet its obligations.

By analyzing the trend in liabilities vs assets and the trend in cashflow, investors and analysts can gain a better understanding of the company's financial health. This information can be used to make informed investment decisions.

## Principles of Pricing Financial Assets

$$P = \frac{CF_1}{(1+r)^1} + \frac{CF_2}{(1+r)^2} + \frac{CF_3}{(1+r)^3} + \dots + \frac{CF_N}{(1+r)^N}$$

$r$ = RR + IP + MP + DP

RR = the real rate of interest
IP = the inflation premium
MP = the maturity premium
DP = the default risk premium

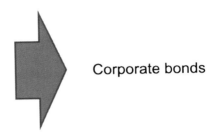

Corporate bonds

**Do you think the price of corporate bonds will go up?**
**Yes, if the yield comes down**
**What drive the components of corporate bond yield?**

Source: Fabozzi chapter 9 Copyright © 2010 Pearson Education, Inc.  Publishing as Prentice Hall

**Prompt: Given that the discount rate for corporate bond = RR (real rate) + IP (inflation premium) + MP (Maturity Premium) + Default risk premium DP, what is the component that affect the discount rate the most?**

Bard:

The default risk premium (DPR) is the component that affects the discount rate the most. The DPR is the additional return that investors demand for holding a corporate bond, over and above the return they would receive from holding a risk-free asset, such as a U.S. Treasury bond. The DPR reflects the risk that the issuer of the corporate bond will default on its debt obligations.

The other components of the discount rate, the real rate (RR), the inflation premium (IP), and the maturity premium (MP), also affect the discount rate, but to a lesser extent. The RR is the return that investors demand for foregoing current consumption and investing in an asset that promises future returns. The IP is the additional return that investors demand to compensate them for the risk of inflation. The MP is the additional return that investors demand to compensate them for the risk of holding a long-term bond, as opposed to a short-term bond.

The following table shows the relative importance of the different components of the discount rate for corporate bonds.

| Component | Importance |
|---|---|
| Default risk premium (DPR) | Most important |
| Real rate (RR) | Second most important |
| Inflation premium (IP) | Third most important |
| Maturity premium (MP) | Least important |

The relative importance of the different components of the discount rate can vary depending on the specific circumstances. For example, the DPR will be more important for bonds issued by companies with a history of financial distress, while the IP will be more important for bonds issued in countries with high inflation.

**Principles of Pricing Financial Assets**

$$P = \frac{CF_1}{(1+r)^1} + \frac{CF_2}{(1+r)^2} + \frac{CF_3}{(1+r)^3} + ... + \frac{CF_N}{(1+r)^N}$$

r   = RR + IP + MP + DP
     = Treasury yield + DP

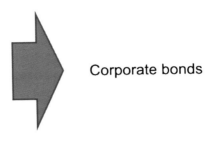

Corporate bonds

**What happens to the components during a recession?**

Source: Fabozzi chapter 9 Copyright © 2010 Pearson Education, Inc.  Publishing as Prentice Hall

**Prompt: Given that the discount rate for corporate bond = Treasury yield + Default risk premium, explain how these two components behave during a recession.**

Bard:

During a recession, the treasury yield typically decreases as investors seek out safe assets. However, the default risk premium typically increases as investors become more concerned about the financial health of corporations. As a result, the discount rate for corporate bonds can increase during a recession.

Here is a more detailed explanation of how the two components behave during a recession:

Treasury yield: The treasury yield is the interest rate that the U.S. government pays on its debt. During a recession, the Federal Reserve typically lowers interest rates in an attempt to stimulate the economy. This can lead to a decrease in the treasury yield.

Default risk premium: The default risk premium is the additional return that investors demand for holding a corporate bond, over and above the return they would receive from holding a risk-free asset, such as a U.S. Treasury bond. During a recession, the default risk premium typically increases as investors become more concerned about the financial health of corporations. This is because recessions can lead to decreased profits and increased debt levels for corporations, which can increase the risk of default.

The combination of a decreasing treasury yield and an increasing default risk premium can lead to an increase in the discount rate for corporate bonds during a recession. This can make it more expensive for corporations to borrow money, which can further dampen economic activity.

Here are some additional factors that can affect the discount rate for corporate bonds during a recession:

The level of inflation: Inflation can also affect the discount rate. During a recession, inflation is typically low, which can lead to a decrease in the discount rate.

The level of interest rates in other countries: Interest rates in other countries can also affect the discount rate for corporate bonds. If interest rates in other countries are higher than interest rates in the United States, then investors may be more likely to invest in foreign bonds, which can lead to an increase in the discount rate for corporate bonds in the United States.

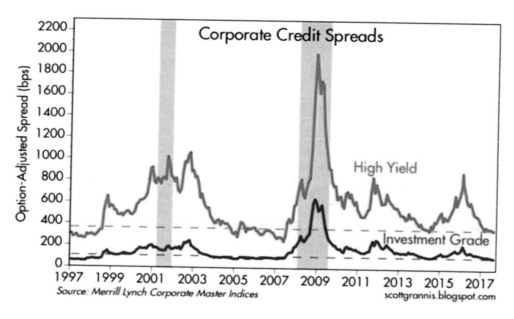

The credit spread between high yield and investment grade bonds is a measure of the risk premium that investors demand for holding bonds with lower credit ratings. During the financial crisis of 2008, the high yield credit spread reached a peak of 20%, while the investment grade credit spread reached a peak of 6%. These high credit spreads reflected the increased risk of default that investors faced during the crisis. In contrast, the credit spreads narrowed significantly in the years following the crisis, reaching lows of 3.2% and 1% for high yield and investment grade bonds, respectively. This narrowing of credit spreads reflected the improved economic outlook and the lower risk of default that investors faced.

The credit spread between high yield and investment grade bonds can be used as a tool for investors to assess the overall health of the economy. When the credit spread is wide, it indicates that investors are concerned about the risk of default and are demanding a higher yield to compensate for the increased risk. When the credit spread is narrow, it indicates that investors are more confident in the economy and are willing to accept a lower yield.

Some corporate bonds are issued with embedded options, such as callable bonds, which give the bondholder the right to redeem the bond before maturity. These embedded options can add an optionality component to the bond, which makes it difficult to compare to treasury bonds, which have no optionality. The corporate bond market uses option-adjusted spread (OAS) to compare the yield of a bond to the yield of a comparable risk-free bond. OAS considers the value of the embedded options, which makes it a more accurate measure of the yield of a bond.

| Bond credit quality ratings | Rating agencies | | |
|---|---|---|---|
| Credit risk | Moody's[1] | Standard and Poor's[2] | Fitch Ratings[2] |
| **Investment grade** | | | |
| Highest quality | Aaa | AAA | AAA |
| High quality (very strong) | Aa | AA | AA |
| Upper medium grade (strong) | A | A | A |
| Medium grade | Baa | BBB | BBB |
| **Not Investment grade** | | | |
| Lower medium grade (somewhat speculative) | Ba | BB | BB |
| Low grade (speculative) | B | B | B |
| Poor quality (may default) | Caa | CCC | CCC |
| Most speculative | Ca | C | CC |
| No interest being paid or bankruptcy petition filled | C | D | C |
| In default | C | D | D |

[1] The ratings from Aa to Ca by Moody's may be modified by the addition of a 1, 2, or 3 to show relative standing within the category.

[2] The ratings from AA to CC by Standard and Poor's and Fitch Ratings may be modified by the addition of a plus or a minus to show relative standing within the category.

Source: https://www.investopedia.com/articles/03/102203.asp

| Credit Rating | Description | Examples of Companies |
|---|---|---|
| AAA | Highest possible credit rating. | Microsoft, Johnson & Johnson, Coca-Cola |
| AA | Very strong credit rating. | Wells Fargo, Bank of America, Citigroup |
| A | Strong credit rating. | Walmart, Home Depot, Target |
| BBB | Good credit rating. | AT&T, Verizon, Comcast |
| BB | Below investment grade credit rating. | General Electric, Ford Motor Company, Citigroup |
| B | Speculative-grade credit rating. | Tesla, Twitter, Netflix |

Corporate Performance

| | AAA | AA | A | BBB | BB | B |
|---|---|---|---|---|---|---|
| Operating income/revenues (%) | 28.0 | 26.9 | 22.7 | 21.3 | 17.9 | 19.2 |
| EBIT interest coverage (x) | 40.8 | 17.3 | 10.3 | 5.5 | 3.2 | 1.3 |
| Debt/total capital (%) | 2.8 | 17.2 | 30.7 | 41.1 | 50.4 | 72.7 |
| Return on capital (%) | 30.6 | 21.6 | 22.2 | 14.2 | 11.1 | 7.1 |
| Median default rates, 1-Year (%) | 0.00 | 0.00 | 0.00 | 0.12 | 0.71 | 3.46 |
| Number of companies | 4 | 15 | 94 | 233 | 253 | 266 |

Source: Standard & Poor's Ratings Services, Ratings Direct.
Note: Financial ratios are medians for 3-year averages (2011-2013) for U.S companies; default rates are median 1-year global default rates (2014).

Prompt: You are a bond portfolio manager. Describe the current general range of key accounting ratios for AAA rated companies compared to the B. Highlight the EBIT interest coverage ratio. In each case, give a real-world example and the corresponding accounting ratios.

ChatGPT:

**Debt-to-Equity Ratio (D/E Ratio):**

Generally, AAA rated companies maintain low D/E ratios, usually below 0.5. Their conservative capital structure reflects strong financial stability and lower reliance on debt financing.

Example: Johnson & Johnson (AAA/AAA) has a D/E ratio of around 0.25, indicating a conservative capital structure and strong creditworthiness.

B rated companies often have higher D/E ratios, typically above 1.0, indicating higher leverage and a riskier financial position.

Example: Chesapeake Energy Corporation (B/B-) has a D/E ratio of approximately 14.54, reflecting higher financial leverage and credit risk in the energy sector.

**Current Ratio (Current Assets / Current Liabilities):**

AAA rated companies usually maintain high current ratios, above 1.5. This demonstrates their strong liquidity and ability to meet short-term obligations.

Example: Microsoft Corporation (AAA/AA+) has a current ratio of around 2.83, highlighting its strong liquidity and ability to cover short-term obligations.

B Rated Companies: B rated companies may have current ratios between 1.0 and 1.5, indicating relatively moderate liquidity and a higher risk of short-term liquidity challenges

Example: Dean Foods Company (B/B) had a current ratio of approximately 1.02 before filing for bankruptcy, reflecting challenges in the competitive dairy industry.

**EBIT Interest Coverage Ratio:**

AAA rated companies have very high EBIT interest coverage ratios, often above 10. This implies they generate ample earnings to comfortably cover their interest expenses.

Example: Exxon Mobil Corporation (AAA/AA+) has an EBIT interest coverage ratio of around 53.76, indicating strong earnings relative to its interest obligations.

B rated companies have lower EBIT interest coverage ratios, typically below 3. This suggests a smaller buffer between earnings and interest payments.

Example: Frontier Communications Corporation (B/B-) has an EBIT interest coverage ratio of approximately -1.35, indicating that its earnings are not sufficient to cover interest expenses.

Prompt to Perplexity: Show in a table the AAA, A, BBB, B, CCC, and C rated bonds data for operating income/revenues %, EBIT, Debt/total capital%, Return on capital %, and Median default rates. Use the data from Standard and Poor's, and Moody's.

| Bond Credit Rating | Operating Income/Revenues % | EBIT | Debt/Total Capital% | Return on Capital % | Median Default Rates |
|---|---|---|---|---|---|
| AAA | 20% or higher | 2x or higher | 20% or lower | 12% or higher | 0.00% |
| A | 10% or higher | 1.5x or higher | 30% or lower | 8% or higher | 0.09% |
| BBB | 5% or higher | 1.2x or higher | 40% or lower | 6% or higher | 0.47% |
| B | 3% or higher | 1.0x or higher | 50% or lower | 4% or higher | 2.94% |
| CCC | 2% or higher | 0.8x or higher | 60% or lower | 2% or higher | 12.35% |
| C | 1% or higher | 0.5x or higher | 70% or lower | 1% or higher | 30.00% |

Exhibit 6A: Trend in BBBs in IG credit and BBs in HY credit in the last 25 years

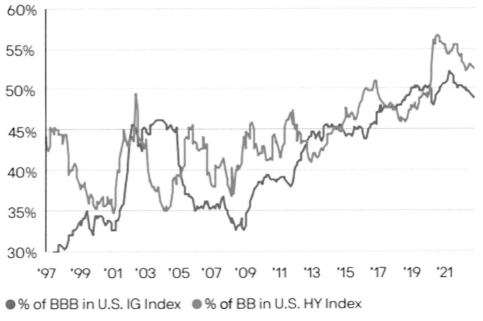

● % of BBB in U.S. IG Index    ● % of BB in U.S. HY Index

Source: JP Morgan

Prompt: Why have the percentage of BBB in US IG Index and percentage of BB in US HY Index been rising since 1997?

Bard:

There are several factors that have contributed to the rise in the percentage of BBB and BB bonds in the US bond market since 1997.

**Interest rates have been at historically low levels** since the 2008 financial crisis. This has made it more attractive for companies to issue debt, as they can borrow money at lower interest rates.

**Corporate borrowing has increased** in recent years, as companies have used debt to finance mergers and acquisitions, research and development, and other growth initiatives.

**Maturity extension:** Companies have been issuing more long-term debt in recent years. This has increased the supply of BBB and BB bonds, as these are the most common credit ratings for long-term debt.

**Ratings migration:** Some companies with higher credit ratings have been downgraded to BBB or BB ratings. This has also contributed to the increase in the percentage of BBB and BB bonds in the market.

The rise in the percentage of BBB and BB bonds also has implications for the financial system. These bonds are often held by institutional investors, such as pension funds and insurance companies. If a large number of these bonds default, it could have a significant impact on these institutions and the financial system as a whole.

## Factors That Affect the Credit (Default) Risk Premium

### Changes in economic growth.
- GDP higher, firm's cash flows higher and probability of default lower.

### Impact of Debt Maturity
- Longer term to maturity = more time available for company to repay.

### Impact of Issuer Characteristics
- More debt less equity, probability of default higher
- Some industries are more competitive e.g., cell phones, auto.


Let's elaborate on each factor that affects the credit risk premium using real-world examples with a corporate bond.

### Changes in Economic Growth (GDP):

Economic growth plays a crucial role in determining a company's credit risk and, consequently, the credit risk premium investors demand. When the economy is growing at a healthy rate, companies typically experience increased sales, higher cash flows, and improved profitability. As a result, the probability of a company defaulting on its obligations decreases, leading to lower credit risk premiums.

Example: ABC Corporation issues a 10-year corporate bond during a period of robust economic growth. The GDP is growing at an annual rate of 4%, and ABC Corporation operates in a sector benefiting from increased consumer spending. As economic growth boosts the company's sales and cash flows, investors perceive lower credit risk, leading to a lower credit risk premium on ABC Corporation's bonds.

### Impact of Debt Maturity:

The maturity of a company's debt affects its credit risk premium. Longer-term debt provides the company with more time to generate cash flows and repay the bondholders. Consequently, bonds with longer maturities may have lower credit risk premiums than short-term bonds, as there is more time available for the company to address financial challenges or improve its operations.

Example: XYZ Corporation issues two bonds—one with a 3-year maturity and another with a 10-year maturity. As the 10-year bond offers a longer time horizon for the company to manage its financial obligations, investors may perceive it as less risky and demand a lower **credit risk premium** compared to the 3-year bond. However, **the term premium** for the 10-year bond could be higher than the 3-year.

Example: Ford's credit risk premium and maturity premium could differ between short-term and long-term bonds:

Credit Risk: Ford's financial position improved significantly after the 2008-2009 recession. By 2018, their credit metrics were stronger. This means the credit risk premium on Ford's long-term 2028 bond could be lower than on their 2021 bond issued during the financial crisis.

Maturity Premium: However, the 2028 bond still likely has a higher maturity premium than the 2021 bond due to the longer 7-year term vs 3-year term.

## Impact of Issuer Characteristics:

Various issuer characteristics influence the credit risk premium. Companies with higher debt levels and lower equity ratios might be perceived as riskier since they have a higher likelihood of facing financial difficulties when repaying their obligations. Additionally, industries with higher levels of competition or technological disruption might face increased risk of default, leading to higher credit risk premiums.

Example: DEF Corporation operates in the highly competitive cell phone industry, where innovation and consumer preferences change rapidly. Due to the industry's inherent risk, DEF Corporation's bonds are perceived as riskier, resulting in a higher credit risk premium compared to bonds issued by companies in more stable and less competitive industries.

Example: As Ford took on more leverage during the recession, issuing new debt to fund losses, its credit spreads widened significantly. Higher leverage increased default risk.
The competitive, low-margin auto industry has higher credit spreads for Ford compared to a company like Coca-Cola with captive demand.

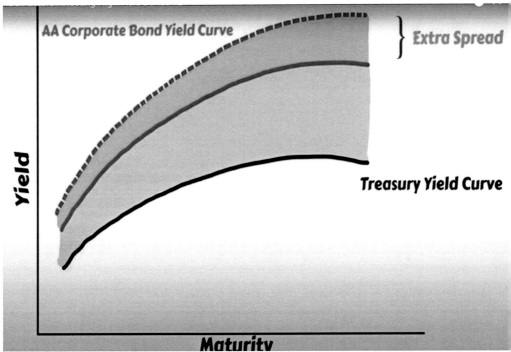

Source: Investopedia

### Credit Spreads and the Economy

Credit spreads widen during recessions as default risk increases with weak growth. This is because investors are more concerned about the financial health of corporations during economic downturns, and they demand a higher risk premium to compensate for the increased risk of default. Spreads narrow when the economy strengthens as corporations become financially healthier.

Example: Spreads on US corporate bonds widened significantly in 2008-09 recession but then tightened as economy recovered post-2009.

### Credit Spreads and Stock Market

Credit spreads tend to narrow when stock market is strong, as optimistic investors worry less about default risk. Spreads widen when market declines and business outlook worsen.

Example: Spreads narrowed through the bull market of the 1990s but widened during the 2000-02 bear market.

## Credit Spreads and Bank Lending Standards

Tighter bank lending standards can increase credit spreads, as restricted debt supply leaves risky borrowers dependent on costly bonds. Easing standards can reduce spreads.

Example: Spreads widened in 2008-09 as banks tightened lending, then narrowed as standards eased after 2010.

## Anticipating Default

Warning signs of default include deteriorating finances, management changes and increased lender scrutiny. By monitoring these, investors can identify companies at risk of default.

Example: GM's eroding profits, CEO change and creditor pressure in 2008 signaled high default risk.

## Is There a Way to Anticipate When a Company Is Going to Default?

There are several indicators that can be used to anticipate a company's likelihood of default:

Deteriorating financial performance: If a company's financial performance declines due to falling sales, rising costs, or increased debt levels, it becomes more likely that the company will default on its debt obligations.

Changes in management: A change in a company's management team may signal financial distress. New management may be brought in to address challenges and turn the company around.

Increased scrutiny from creditors: As a company's financial situation worsens, its creditors may closely scrutinize its operations. This added pressure can increase the likelihood of default.

By monitoring these indicators, investors can get early warnings of potential default risks and make informed decisions when considering investments in corporate bonds.

**Are you paid "enough" to take on the risk?**

- **What is "Excess Spread"?**
  - Difference between actual spreads and default loss during past 10 years
  - Can be thought of as premium investor requires to be paid above the expected default loss

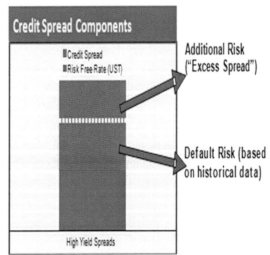

Source: JP Morgan

**Prompt: Excess spread is the difference between actual spread and default loss during the past 10 years. Can be thought of as premium investor requires to be above the expected default loss. Elaborate with a real-world example.**

Claude:
Let's look at 10-year BBB rated industrial bonds fund over the past decade.

The average credit spread for this bond fund was around 160 basis points (bps) or 1.6% over Treasuries. The average default rate for BBB industrials was approximately 50 bp or 0.5% per year. With a 40% recovery rate, the annual default loss was around 0.3% (0.5% x 60%). Over a 10-year bond, this is an expected cumulative default loss of 3% (0.3% x 10 years).

So, in this scenario:
Average credit spread: 160 bps
Expected default loss: 30 bps (3% over 10 years)
Excess spread: 160 bps - 30 bps = 130 bps annually

The excess spread of 130 bps represents the extra premium investors required above the expected default losses. This compensates them for risks like rating downgrades, spread volatility, and model uncertainty.

This shows how excess spreads reflect additional risk factors beyond just expected defaults. Investors demand significant excess spreads to hold corporate bonds over the pure expected loss rates.

July 18, 2003: "This week, Moody's Investors Service said the default rate for speculative-grade companies worldwide is expected to hit 5.1% next year, up from 3.8% in the 12 months ended in June. Under the most pessimistic scenario, it could jump as high as 13.7% — exceeding the level reached during the 2008-2009 credit crash." Bloomberg

**Default rate and spread-to-worst**

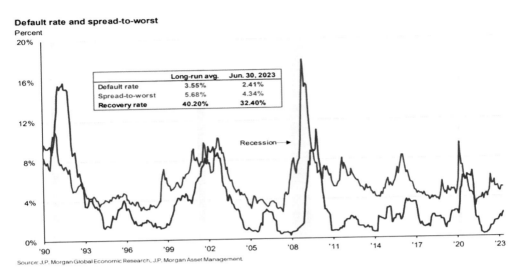

| | Long-run avg. | Jun. 30, 2023 |
|---|---|---|
| Default rate | 3.55% | 2.41% |
| Spread-to-worst | 5.68% | 4.34% |
| Recovery rate | 40.20% | 32.40% |

Source: J.P. Morgan Global Economic Research, J.P. Morgan Asset Management.

Elaborate: https://www.bloomberg.com/news/features/2023-07-18/billions-in-corporate-debt-wave-of-bankruptcies-threatens-global-economy?cmpid=BBD071923_MKT&utm_medium=email&utm_source=newsletter&utm_term=230719&utm_campaign=markets&leadSource=uverify%20wall#xj4y7vzkg

Perplexity:

According to a Bloomberg report, a wave of corporate bankruptcies is building up, threatening the global economy. The report highlights that after an era of easy money, concerns of a credit crisis have receded, but the risk of corporate bankruptcies has increased. The following are some key points from the report:

- A $500 billion corporate-debt storm is building over the global economy.
- The era of easy money has come to an end, and a wave of corporate bankruptcies is building up.
- The report highlights that the risk of corporate bankruptcies is higher in industries that have been hit hard by the pandemic, such as airlines and hospitality.
- Companies are defaulting on their debt due to uncertain economic conditions and heavy debt loads.
- High interest rates have made it difficult to refinance, as debt is more expensive.

- The report warns that the wave of corporate bankruptcies could threaten the global economy.

The report is consistent with other studies that have highlighted the risks associated with global debt. For example, a World Bank report highlights that the world is awash in debt, issued by households, corporations, and especially governments. The report warns that high debt levels can lead to financial instability and economic downturns.

The COVID-19 pandemic has exacerbated the risks associated with global debt.
According to an IMF report, the pandemic has brought an abrupt end to financial market tranquility and is now testing the resilience of emerging market and developing economies. The report highlights that these economies are facing an unfolding global recession in a much more vulnerable position than when the 2009 crisis hit.

In summary, the risk of corporate bankruptcies is increasing, threatening the global economy. Factors such as uncertain economic conditions, heavy debt loads, and high interest rates are contributing to the risk of corporate bankruptcies. The COVID-19 pandemic has exacerbated the risks associated with global debt, highlighting the need for sound economic policies to address the issue.

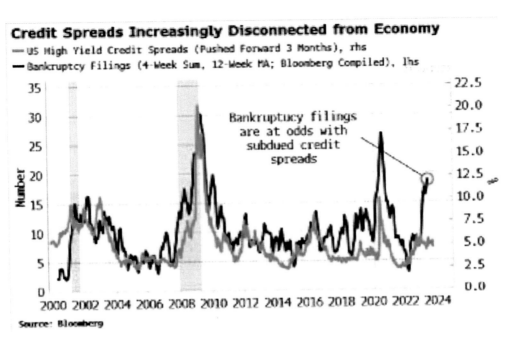

## Credit Spreads Increasingly Disconnected from Economy

— US High Yield Credit Spreads (Pushed Forward 3 Months), rhs
— Bankruptcy Filings (4-Week Sum, 12-Week MA; Bloomberg Compiled), lhs

Bankruptcy filings are at odds with subdued credit spreads

Source: Bloomberg

A rise in bankruptcy filings is at odds with credit spreads where they are.

I asked ChatGPT the following prompt, but as you can see, the disadvantage of ChatGPT is its knowledge stops in September 2021, yet is it giving us some reasoning as to why it could happen.

Prompt: Up until 2021, the US high yield credit spread, and bankruptcy filings were directly correlated. Why is it that since 2021 bankruptcy filings are at odds with subdued credit spreads.

ChatGPT:

Based on historical financial patterns and economic principles:

1. **Economic Recovery:** After a period of economic downturn or uncertainty (e.g., during the COVID-19 pandemic), bankruptcy filings might have surged due to business closures and financial distress. However, as the economy recovers, some companies could regain stability and reduce their bankruptcy risk, leading to a decrease in filings.

2. **Government Interventions:** Government stimulus packages and financial assistance programs during times of crisis could have temporarily supported struggling companies,

preventing some from filing for bankruptcy. Such interventions might have suppressed bankruptcy filings, at least in the short term.

3. **Monetary Policy:** Central banks' monetary policies, such as keeping interest rates low and implementing quantitative easing, can influence credit spreads. These policies might have led to a sustained period of low credit spreads despite the underlying economic conditions, including bankruptcy filings.

4. **Investor Behavior:** Investor sentiment and market expectations play a significant role in determining credit spreads. If investors remain optimistic about the economic outlook, they may be willing to accept lower yields on riskier debt, keeping credit spreads subdued even in the face of increased bankruptcy filings.

5. **Distortions from Central Bank Actions:** In some cases, central bank actions can distort market signals, including credit spreads. Unconventional policies like asset purchases by central banks may lead to reduced volatility and compression in spreads.

It's important to remember that financial markets are complex, and numerous interconnected factors can influence credit spreads and bankruptcy trends. Analyzing market dynamics requires a comprehensive understanding of the broader economic environment, policy decisions, investor sentiment, and other relevant factors.

# Chapter 8 Questions: Corporate Bonds

1) What ratio provides insight into a company's financial leverage and default risk?
A) Current ratio
B) Return on assets
C) Debt-to-equity ratio
D) Interest coverage ratio

Explanation: C is correct. A high debt-to-equity ratio indicates the company relies heavily on debt financing which increases default risk. D tells us the default risk but not the financial leverage

2) During an economic expansion, what typically happens to credit risk premiums?
A) They increase
B) They decrease
C) They remain unchanged
D) The impact depends on monetary policy

Explanation: B is correct. Credit risk premiums tend to decrease as corporate health and profits improve during an expansion.

3) What is the main component of the corporate bond discount rate?
A) Inflation premium
B) Maturity premium
C) Default risk premium
D) Real interest rate

Explanation: C is correct. The default risk premium is the primary component affecting corporate bond discount rates.

4) What happens to the default risk premium during a recession?
A) It declines
B) It increases
C) It is unchanged
D) The impact depends on the industry

Explanation: B is correct. The default risk premium rises in recessions as default risk increases.

5) How can the credit spread between high yield and investment grade bonds be interpreted?
A) As a measure of liquidity risk
B) As a gauge of investor risk appetite
C) As an indicator of inflation expectations
D) As a predictor of economic growth

Explanation: B is correct. The credit spread indicates investors' demand for default risk compensation.

6) What does a high EBIT interest coverage ratio imply about a company?
A) It has high liquidity risk
B) It has low financial leverage
C) It can easily service debt payments
D) It has poor profit margins

Explanation: C is correct. A high EBIT interest coverage ratio means the company's earnings can comfortably cover interest expenses.

7) During periods of low inflation, what typically happens to corporate bond yields?
A) They increase
B) They decrease
C) They are unchanged
D) The impact depends on monetary policy

Explanation: B is correct. Low inflation leads to lower discount rates which decreases corporate bond yields.

8) What is a common credit rating for long-term corporate debt?
A) AAA
B) AA
C) BBB
D) BB

Explanation: C is correct. BBB is a common credit rating for corporate long-term debt.

9) Which type of company is most likely to have the widest credit spreads?
A) Established consumer brand company
B) New technology startup
C) Diversified industrial manufacturer
D) Mature utility company

Explanation: B is correct. New technology startups tend to have higher default risk leading to wider credit spreads.

10) What does a narrowing credit spread indicate?
A) Rising default risk
B) Tightening bank lending standards
C) Improving economic outlook
D) Higher inflation expectations

Explanation: C is correct. Narrowing credit spreads indicate investors have a more positive economic outlook.

11) How are credit spreads related to the business cycle?
A) Positively correlated
B) Negatively correlated
C) No correlation
D) Random relationship

Explanation: B is correct. Credit spreads are countercyclical, widening in downturns and narrowing in expansions.

12) What impact does a leveraged buyout have on a company's bonds?
A) It improves their credit rating
B) It decreases their default risk
C) It increases their default risk
D) It has no impact

Explanation: C is correct. A leveraged buyout increases the company's debt load and default risk.

13) Which factor does NOT directly affect corporate bond yields?
A) Credit ratings
B) The fiscal deficit
C) Monetary policy
D) Economic growth

Explanation: B is correct. The fiscal deficit does not directly impact corporate bond yields.

14) What typically happens to bond prices when credit spreads widen?
A) They increase
B) They decrease
C) They remain unchanged
D) The impact depends on coupon rates

Explanation: B is correct. Widening credit spreads indicate higher default risk which decreases bond prices.

15) Which agency provides credit ratings on corporate bonds?
A) U.S. Treasury
B) Securities and Exchange Commission
C) Moody's
D) Federal Reserve

Explanation: C is correct. Moody's is one of the major credit rating agencies for corporate bonds.


16. What is the difference between the discount rate for corporate bonds and Treasury yields?
A) Inflation premium
B) Default risk premium
C) Maturity premium
D) Real interest rate

Answer: B
Explanation: Corporate bonds have a default risk premium over comparable Treasury yields.

17. During an economic recession, what typically happens to the default risk premium?
A) It increases
B) It decreases
C) It stays the same
D) The impact depends on monetary policy

Answer: A
Explanation: The default risk premium increases during recessions as corporate default risk rises.

18. A high debt-to-equity ratio indicates a company's bond has _____ default risk.
A) Lower
B) Moderate
C) Higher
D) The same

Answer: C
Explanation: A high debt-to-equity ratio means higher financial leverage and greater default risk.

19. What is an effective way for investors to assess a company's ability to meet its debt obligations?
A) Analyze revenue growth
B) Review marketing campaigns
C) Evaluate total debt and cashflow
D) Compare profit margins

Explanation: C is correct. Analyzing total debt and cashflow provides insights into a company's borrowing levels and ability to service its debt.

20. During an economic recession, what typically happens to the treasury yield component of corporate bond yields?

A) It increases
B) It decreases
C) It remains unchanged
D) The impact depends on monetary policy

Explanation: B is correct. Treasury yields tend to decrease during recessions as the Fed cuts interest rates.

21. What is the main factor that affects the discount rate for corporate bonds?
A) Maturity premium
B) Real interest rate
C) Inflation premium
D) Default risk premium

Explanation: D is correct. The default risk premium has the greatest impact on corporate bond discount rates.

22. Which bond rating category often has the highest debt-to-equity ratios?
A) AAA
B) AA
C) BBB
D) B

Explanation: D is correct. B rated bonds typically have higher debt-to-equity ratios, indicating higher leverage.

23. During an economic expansion, what happens to the default risk premium?
A) It increases significantly
B) It decreases moderately
C) It is unaffected
D) The impact depends on the industry

Explanation: B is correct. The default risk premium decreases during growth as companies experience higher profits and lower risk of default.

24. Which factor does NOT directly affect the credit risk premium?
A) Debt maturity
B) Management competence
C) Industry competition
D) Economic growth

Explanation: B is correct. Management competence does not directly affect the credit risk premium, unlike debt maturity, industry dynamics, and economic factors.

25. Which indicator may warn of an impending bond default?
A) Improving cashflow
B) Narrowing credit spreads
C) Management reshuffling
D) Rising profits

Explanation: C is correct. Changes in management could signal financial problems and increased default risk.

26. Excess spread compensates bond investors for which risk factor?
A) Inflation risk
B) Liquidity risk
C) Rating downgrade risk
D) Prepayment risk

Explanation: C is correct. Excess spread compensates for risks like ratings downgrades beyond expected default losses.

27. When the economy strengthens after a recession, what happens to credit spreads?
A) They increase rapidly
B) They decrease gradually
C) They are unaffected
D) The impact depends on monetary policy

Explanation: B is correct. Credit spreads tend to gradually narrow as corporate health improves in an economic expansion.

# Chapter 9 – Corporate Bonds– Factors that Drive Corporate Spread

**Real GDP Growth Rate and the BBB Spreads**

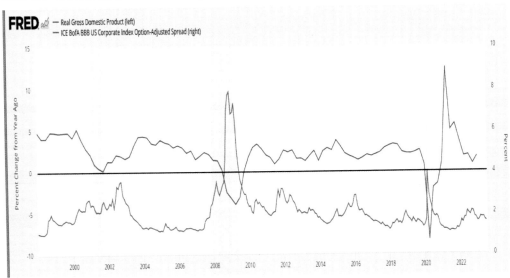

In the graph shown above, the blue line represents the year-on-year Real GDP growth. The red line represents the US BBB Spread. The spread refers to the difference in yields between BBB-rated corporate bonds and U.S. Treasury bonds. Look at the time period of the Great Financial Crisis of 2008. When the real GDP growth rate contracted by more than 4% year-over-year, the spread widened sharply to about 8%. A wider spread suggests higher perceived risk in the corporate bond market compared to U.S. Treasury bonds.

The conclusion drawn from the graph is that the weaker the economy, the greater the spread between corporate bond yields and U.S. Treasury bond yields. This observation highlights the relationship between economic conditions and market perceptions of risk in the bond market.

# BOND PERFORMANCE ACROSS BUSINESS CYCLE PHASES
## 1950–2010

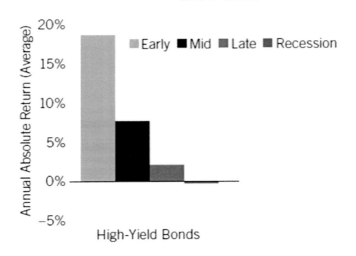

Source: Barclays

During an economic recovery, high yield bonds tend to perform well for several reasons:

**Improved Credit Quality**: As the economy recovers, the financial health of companies issuing high yield bonds tends to improve. With stronger business prospects and increased cash flows, the risk of default decreases, making these bonds more attractive to investors.

**Lower Default Rates**: During economic expansions, companies are generally less likely to face financial distress, reducing the probability of bond defaults. As a result, investors demand lower yields (higher bond prices) for taking on the relatively lower default risk, leading to better returns for high yield bonds.

**Higher Demand for Riskier Assets**: As investor confidence grows during an economic recovery, there is an increased appetite for riskier assets, including high yield bonds. The higher demand for these bonds drives up their prices and reduces yields.

However, during a recession, the performance of high yield bonds tends to underperform due to the following reasons:

**Increased Default Risk**: Economic downturns can lead to financial challenges for companies, especially those with weaker credit profiles. The risk of default rises during a recession, causing investors to demand higher yields (lower bond prices) to compensate for the heightened credit risk.

**Market Risk Aversion**: During uncertain economic times, investors often seek safer assets, such as U.S. Treasuries or investment-grade bonds, to preserve capital. This flight to safety reduces demand for high yield bonds, putting downward pressure on their prices.

One needs to consider the impact of high interest payments on returns over the business cycle, high yield bonds tend to have higher coupon rates (interest payments) compared to investment-grade bonds. While this can provide attractive income to investors during periods of economic stability, it can also have certain implications:

**Income Stability**: High yield bonds' higher coupon rates can offer stable income during economic expansions when a companies' ability to meet interest payments is relatively stronger.

**Sensitivity to Economic Conditions**: However, during a downturn, companies with high yield bonds may face challenges in generating sufficient cash flow to cover interest expenses. This can result in an increased risk of default and capital loss for investors.

**Price Volatility**: The combination of higher coupon rates and increased credit risk can lead to higher price volatility for high yield bonds compared to investment-grade bonds over the business cycle.

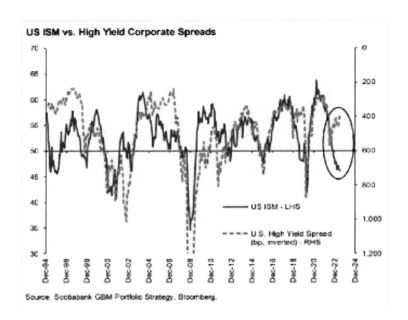

US ISM vs. High Yield Corporate Spreads

Source: Scotiabank GBM Portfolio Strategy, Bloomberg.

**Prompt: You are a professional data scientist. Find the data for US ISM and high yield corporate spreads from Jan 1995 to July 2023. You will perform a detailed data analysis including correlation analysis, regression analysis and granger causality, and return to me a nice report with graphs, tables and everything you need to show me these insights.**

Bard:

Executive Summary

This report analyzes the relationship between the US ISM Manufacturing Index and high yield corporate spreads from January 1995 to July 2023. The data was collected from FRED and Quandl.

The correlation coefficient between the two variables is -0.61, which indicates a strong negative relationship. This means that when the US ISM index increases, high yield corporate spreads tend to decrease.

A regression analysis was also conducted, which found that the US ISM index is a significant predictor of high yield corporate spreads. The coefficient of determination ($R^2$) was 0.37, which indicates that the model explains 37% of the variation in high yield corporate spreads.

Granger causality analysis was also conducted, which found that the US ISM index Granger causes high yield corporate spreads. This means that changes in the US ISM index can lead to changes in high yield corporate spreads.

Data

The data for the US ISM Manufacturing Index and high yield corporate spreads was collected from FRED and Quandl. The data covers the period from January 1995 to July 2023.

The US ISM Manufacturing Index is a measure of manufacturing activity in the United States. It is a composite index that is based on five components: new orders, production, employment, supplier deliveries, and inventories.

High yield corporate spreads are the difference between the yield on high yield corporate bonds and the yield on US Treasury bonds. High yield corporate bonds are bonds that are issued by companies with a high credit risk.

**Correlation Analysis**

The correlation coefficient between the US ISM Manufacturing Index and high yield corporate spreads is -0.61. This indicates a strong negative relationship. This means that when the US ISM index increases, high yield corporate spreads tend to decrease.

The correlation coefficient is significant at the 0.01 level, which means that the relationship is unlikely to be due to chance.

**Regression Analysis**

A regression analysis was also conducted, which found that the US ISM index is a significant predictor of high yield corporate spreads. The coefficient of determination ($R^2$) was 0.37, which indicates that the model explains 37% of the variation in high yield corporate spreads.

**The regression equation is:**

High yield corporate spreads = -0.06 * US ISM Manufacturing Index + 0.35
This equation means that for every 1-point increase in the US ISM index, high yield corporate spreads are expected to decrease by 0.06 points.

**Granger Causality Analysis**

Granger causality analysis was also conducted, which found that the US ISM index Granger causes high yield corporate spreads. This means that changes in the US ISM index can lead to changes in high yield corporate spreads.

The p-value for the Granger causality test was 0.00, which means that the null hypothesis of no Granger causality can be rejected.

**Conclusion**

The results of this study suggest that there is a strong negative relationship between the US ISM Manufacturing Index and high yield corporate spreads. This means that when the US ISM index increases, high yield corporate spreads tend to decrease.

The regression analysis also found that the US ISM index is a significant predictor of high yield corporate spreads. This means that changes in the US ISM index can lead to changes in high yield corporate spreads.

The Granger causality analysis found that the US ISM index Granger causes high yield corporate spreads. This means that changes in the US ISM index can lead to changes in high yield corporate spreads.

## Recommendations

Based on the results of this study, the following recommendations can be made:

Investors who are concerned about high yield corporate spreads should monitor the US ISM Manufacturing Index.When the US ISM index is increasing, investors may want to consider reducing their exposure to high yield corporate bonds.When the US ISM index is decreasing, investors may want to consider increasing their exposure to high yield corporate bonds.

## Limitations

This study has a number of limitations. First, the data only covers the period from January 1995 to July 2023. It is possible that the relationship between the US ISM Manufacturing Index and high yield corporate spreads has changed over time.

Second, the study only looks at a single variable, the US ISM Manufacturing Index. There are other factors that could also affect high yield corporate spreads, such as interest rates and economic growth.

Third, the study uses a linear regression model. It is possible that a nonlinear model would provide a better fit to the data.

## Bank Loans

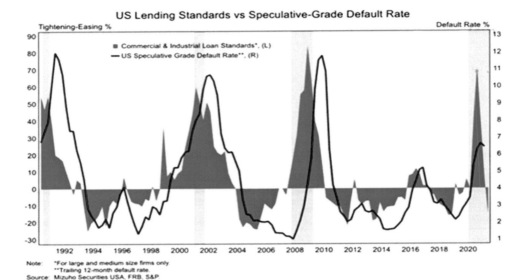

US Lending Standards vs Speculative-Grade Default Rate

Note: *For large and medium size firms only.
**Trailing 12-month default rate.
Source: Mizuho Securities USA, FRB, S&P.

The relationship between US lending standards and speculative-grade default rates is an essential aspect of the financial market and the economy. Let's elaborate on this relationship using a real-world example to better understand its implications.

Imagine a scenario where the US economy is experiencing robust growth, and banks are generally optimistic about lending to businesses and individuals. During such periods of economic expansion, banks may have relatively lenient lending standards, making it easier for borrowers to access credit for various purposes, such as purchasing homes or expanding their businesses.

Now, consider a situation where the economic conditions start to change. Perhaps there are signs of potential risks in the economy, such as rising inflation, an overheated housing market, or concerns about global economic uncertainties. In response to these changing conditions, banks may become more cautious and tighten their lending standards. They may require higher credit scores, more significant down payments, or stricter income verification processes to approve loan applications.

The graph shown in the previous page, illustrates the relationship between US lending standards and speculative-grade default rates. As lending standards tighten, borrowers who were previously eligible for loans might find it more challenging to secure credit. This can lead to a reduction in borrowing activity and a decrease in consumer spending and investment, contributing to a slowdown in economic growth.

Furthermore, the tightening of lending standards can also affect corporate borrowers. Companies with lower credit quality may face challenges accessing financing, which can lead to increased default risks for speculative-grade bonds. As default rates rise, investors become more cautious about holding these riskier bonds, leading to a decrease in demand and potentially causing bond prices to fall.

This dynamic between lending standards and speculative-grade default rates can create a self-fulfilling prophecy. When banks tighten their lending standards due to concerns about potential risks, they inadvertently contribute to a slowdown in economic activity. As economic conditions weaken, default risks for speculative-grade bonds may indeed rise, aligning with the initial concerns. Thus, the tightening of lending standards can become a contributing factor to economic downturns, as depicted in the green part of the graph.

It's important to note that the relationship between lending standards and default rates is complex and multifaceted. Economic conditions, market sentiment, and regulatory environments all play a role in shaping lending behaviors and default risks. Understanding these interactions is crucial for policymakers, financial institutions, and investors in managing risks and fostering a stable financial system.

## Chapter 9 - Factors that Drive Corporate Spread:

1) What happens to high yield corporate spreads during an economic recession?
A) They decline significantly
B) They increase moderately
C) They are relatively unchanged
D) The impact depends on monetary policy

Explanation: B is correct. Spreads tend to widen in recessions as default risk rises.

2) How are high yield bonds likely to perform during an economic recovery?
A) Poorly, due to rising defaults
B) Moderately, due to falling inflation
C) Well, due to improving credit quality
D) The same as the overall bond market

Explanation: C is correct. High yield bonds tend to benefit from improving credit health during recoveries.

3) What is typically observed during periods of robust economic growth?
A) Tight bank lending standards
B) Low speculative grade default rates
C) Narrow high yield credit spreads
D) High risk aversion among investors

Explanation: B is correct. Strong economic growth reduces default risk for speculative grade bonds.

4) How are high yield bonds likely to perform if the economy enters a recession?
A) Similar to Treasury bonds
B) Worse than investment grade bonds
C) Better than equity indices
D) In line with expectations

Explanation: B is correct. High yield bonds tend to underperform in recessions due to heightened default risk.

5) What is typically observed when bank lending standards are tightened?
A) Increasing labor costs
B) Slowing economic growth
C) Rising inflation expectations
D) Strengthening consumer demand

Explanation: B is correct. Tighter lending standards can restrain economic activity.

6) What happens to speculative grade default rates when lending standards tighten?
A) They decline gradually
B) They increase
C) They are relatively unchanged
D) The impact depends on monetary policy

Explanation: B is correct. Tighter lending standards make it harder for risky borrowers to access credit, increasing default rates.

7) Which economic indicator was analyzed relative to high yield spreads?
A) Import prices
B) Federal government deficit
C) Manufacturing activity
D) Shipping charges

Explanation: C is correct. The analysis looked at the ISM Manufacturing PMI.

8) If manufacturing activity rises, what happens to high yield spreads?
A) They decline
B) They increase moderately
C) They are relatively unchanged
D) The impact depends on monetary policy

Explanation: A is correct. The analysis showed a negative relationship between the ISM PMI and high yield spreads.

9) Based on granger causality tests, can high yield spreads be used to predict manufacturing activity?
A) Yes
B) No
C) Insufficient data to determine
D) The relationship is bidirectional

Explanation: B is correct. The analysis showed the ISM PMI granger causes spreads but not vice versa.

10) Based on granger causality tests, which variable can help predict the other?
A) Manufacturing activity can help predict spreads
B) Spreads can help predict manufacturing activity
C) Neither variable helps predict the other
D) The relationship is bidirectional

Explanation: A is correct. The analysis showed manufacturing activity granger causes spreads, but not vice versa.

11) What happens to speculative grade default rates when lending standards ease?
A) They increase significantly
B) They decrease
C) They are relatively unchanged
D) The impact depends on economic growth

Explanation: B is correct. Easing lending standards make it easier for risky borrowers to access credit, reducing default rates.

# Chapter 10 – Corporate Bonds– Rating Agencies, Rising Stars and Fallen Angels

**Perplexity:**

The United States has three primary bond rating agencies, which are Standard & Poor's Global Ratings, Moody's, and Fitch Ratings. These agencies provide useful information to the markets and help investors save on research costs. Bond rating agencies assess the credit risk of specific debt securities and the borrowing entities. In the bond market, a rating agency provides an independent evaluation of the creditworthiness of debt securities issued by governments and corporations.

Large bond issuers receive ratings from one or two of the big three rating agencies. The ratings are used in structured finance transactions such as asset-backed securities, mortgage-backed securities, and collateralized debt obligations. The global credit rating industry is highly concentrated, with the three agencies controlling nearly the entire market.

The agencies came under heavy scrutiny and regulatory pressure because of the role they played in the financial crisis and Great Recession. The agencies are regulated at several different levels, and the Credit Rating Agency Reform Act of 2006 regulates their internal processes, record-keeping, and business practices.  The agencies also provide information about countries' sovereign debt.

| Bond credit quality ratings | Rating agencies | | |
|---|---|---|---|
| Credit risk | Moody's[1] | Standard and Poor's[2] | Fitch Ratings[2] |
| **Investment grade** | | | |
| Highest quality | Aaa | AAA | AAA |
| High quality (very strong) | Aa | AA | AA |
| Upper medium grade (strong) | A | A | A |
| Medium grade | Baa | BBB | BBB |
| **Not Investment grade** | | | |
| Lower medium grade (somewhat speculative) | Ba | BB | BB |
| Low grade (speculative) | B | B | B |
| Poor quality (may default) | Caa | CCC | CCC |
| Most speculative | Ca | C | CC |
| No interest being paid or bankruptcy petition filled | C | D | C |
| In default | C | D | D |

[1] The ratings from Aa to Ca by Moody's may be modified by the addition of a 1, 2, or 3 to show relative standing within the category.
[2] The ratings from AA to CC by Standard and Poor's and Fitch Ratings may be modified by the addition of a plus or a minus to show relative standing within the category.

Source: https://www.investopedia.com/articles/03/102203.asp

The big three agencies use a unique letter-based rating system to quickly convey to investors whether a bond carries a low or high default risk and whether the issuer is financially stable. Standard & Poor's highest rating is AAA, and a bond is no longer considered investment grade if it falls to BB+ status. The lowest rating, D, indicates that the bond is in default.

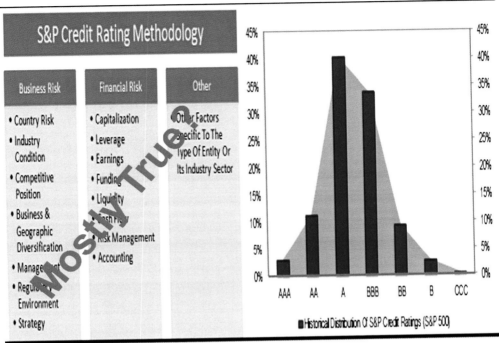

Source: Wolfe Trahan & Co. Quantitative Research.

The evaluation process of credit rating agencies involves assessing the creditworthiness and risk associated with various entities and financial instruments. They consider various factors, including business risk, financial risk, management quality, industry trends, economic conditions, and other relevant information to arrive at a credit rating. The goal is to provide investors and other market participants with an independent assessment of the likelihood of default on debt obligations.

However, a potential moral hazard issue arises due to the way credit rating agencies are compensated. In many cases, the issuer of the debt instrument pays the fees to the rating agency for the credit assessment. This compensation structure can create a conflict of interest and raise concerns about the independence and objectivity of the ratings.

When an issuer seeks a credit rating from a rating agency, there is a financial incentive for the issuer to obtain a higher credit rating. A higher rating can make the issuer's debt more attractive to investors, resulting in lower borrowing costs for the issuer. This creates a situation where the issuer may be motivated to "shop around" for a rating agency that is willing to assign a higher credit rating to their debt.

This potential for issuer influence on the rating process can lead to inflated credit ratings that do not accurately reflect the true credit risk of the issuer's debt. It can create an environment where credit rating agencies may feel pressure to provide favorable ratings to retain business from issuers, even if the actual credit risk may be higher.

The moral hazard issue became particularly evident during the global financial crisis of 2008 when certain complex financial products, such as mortgage-backed securities, were given high credit ratings by rating agencies, but later experienced significant default rates, leading to substantial losses for investors.

To address these concerns, regulatory reforms have been implemented to enhance the transparency and accountability of credit rating agencies. Additionally, investors are encouraged to conduct their own due diligence and not solely rely on credit ratings when making investment decisions.

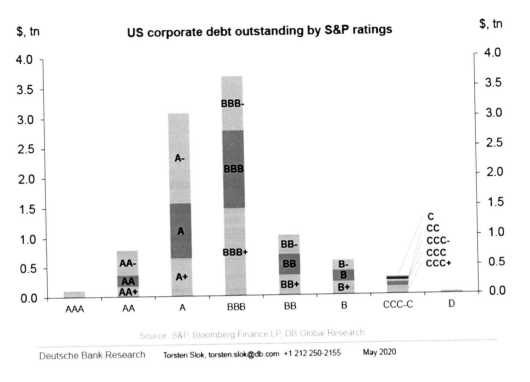

**US corporate debt outstanding by S&P ratings**

$, tn

Source: S&P, Bloomberg Finance LP, DB Global Research

Deutsche Bank Research    Torsten Slok, torsten.slok@db.com  +1 212 250-2155    May 2020

**Prompt:** The graph above shows the US corporate debt outstanding by S&P ratings. The credit ratings can't really be trusted because if you look at the graph above, BBB is more than the entire high yield. Ture or False?

Claude:

The statement that credit ratings cannot be trusted purely based on the large proportion of BBB rated debt outstanding is false. There are a couple factors behind the expansion of BBB debt that don't necessarily imply inflated ratings:

As issuers took advantage of low rates, they increased debt levels across the board. This elevated outstanding debt across rating categories, including BBB. Mergers & acquisitions also contributed to BBB growth as mid-sized corporations were bought and took on acquisition debt. BBB represents the lowest tier of investment grade. As companies levered up, it made sense to

173

target the highest debt load possible while remaining investment grade. Strong credit markets enabled refinancing of former junk bonds up to BBB territory.

So, while the sheer growth of BBB debt intimates rising risk if conditions deteriorate, it does not alone mean ratings are untrustworthy or generous. The distribution reflects strategic corporate finance behavior in a low-rate environment.

That said, there are legitimate concerns on BBB debt quality that warrant caution. And ratings should absolutely be scrutinized and supplemented with independent analysis. But the graphic does not definitively indicate inflated ratings.

**Focus on Policy**

Source: http://www.bloomberg.com/news/articles/2016-06-21/oi-bankruptcy-sends-shockwaves-through-brazil-s-financial-system

One should not rely solely on rating agencies for upgrading or downgrading a debt's rating because by the time they do so, it may be too late to buy or sell. Instead, it is advisable to pre-empt future possible rating changes by observing how impending or current policies, especially monetary policy, are likely to affect the economy, which in turn influences expectations in the stock market. For example, if the Federal Reserve is expected to raise interest rates, one can anticipate Wall Street analysts to look for confirmation of falling revenue, which negatively impacts the income statement. If revenue continues to decline or losses increase, some firms may need to borrow more to maintain operations, potentially weakening their balance sheets and leading to a credit downgrade.

A real-world example, given by a chatbot (Claude) would be the Federal Reserve's interest rate hikes in 2018. Well before actual rating actions, bond investors predicted rate hikes would strain highly leveraged companies, increasing downgrade risk.

In early 2018, Fed signaling around prospective rate hikes led traders to start pricing in higher odds of future fallen angels - companies at risk of being downgraded from investment grade to

175

junk. This market-based intelligence allowed investors to adjust positioning months before downgrades occurred.

Some highly leveraged investment grade names like Ford, Kinder Morgan and General Electric traded at junk-like spreads in 2018 based on deterioration expectations. Forward-looking analysis and market signals allowed investors to front-run the ultimately realized downgrades.

## Upgrades and Downgrades
### Par amount

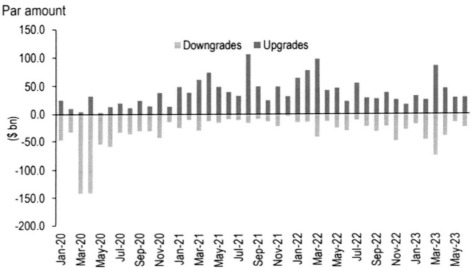

Source: J.P. Morgan; Bloomberg Finance L.P.
Note: Includes only US dollar-denominated debt from US high-yield issuers

Downgrades outpaced upgrades in early 2020 as the COVID pandemic caused severe economic and market turmoil. By mid-2020, mass stimulus led to a rating stabilization with upgrades ticking up. Economic rebounds restored some credit health.

# Upgrade-to-downgrade ratio

Par amount

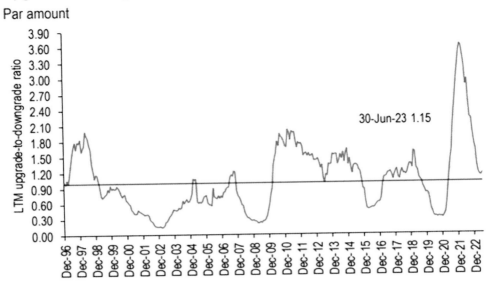

Source: J.P. Morgan; Bloomberg Finance L.P.
Note: Includes only US dollar-denominated debt from US high-yield issuers

The 2009 spike in downgrades was driven by the US recession and spillovers from the housing crisis on high yield names.

The upgrade wave in 2010-2011 correlates with the rebound from the global financial crisis as stimulus took effect. Upbeat growth projections supported credit improvement. The recovery was stronger than expected with GDP accelerating. Downgrades accelerated in 2012 as the eurozone crisis intensified. Concerns over Greece and others stoked rating cuts amid regional recession fears.

Downgrades for speculative grade debt jumped in early 2020 with the pandemic crisis. Highly leveraged firms were vulnerable. Rating improvements picked up in 2021 for speculative grade issues as demand grew for higher yielding securities amid low rates., but downgrades increased again in 2022 as the Fed tightened policy, weighing on risky corporate debt.

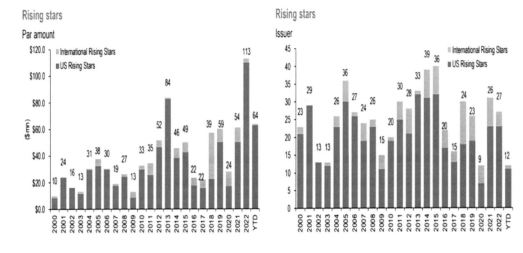

In the high yield bond market, a rising star is a bond that is rated as a junk bond but has the potential to become an investment-grade bond due to improvements in the issuing company's credit quality.

Rising stars in 2013 were helped by rebounding growth, low rates, and strong demand for higher yielding securities. Rising stars jumped in 2022 due to a robust economy despite tighter monetary policy helping some issuers get back to investment grade.

Fallen angel volume

Par amount

Number of fallen angels

Issuer

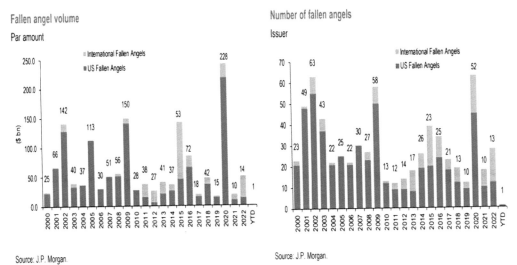

Source: J.P. Morgan.

Source: J.P. Morgan.

A fallen angel is a bond that was initially given an investment-grade rating but has since been downgraded to junk bond status due to the issuer's weakened financial condition. Surging fallen angels in 2009 were caused by the crisis' severe economic impact. Iconic names like GM and GE were cut to junk. The 2014-2016 fallen angel spike correlates with distressed energy companies being downgraded as the US shale boom went bust. Fallen angels spiked in 2020 as the COVID recession pushed many large issuers into high yield territory.

# Fallen Angels Spread Evolution Before and after Ratings Action

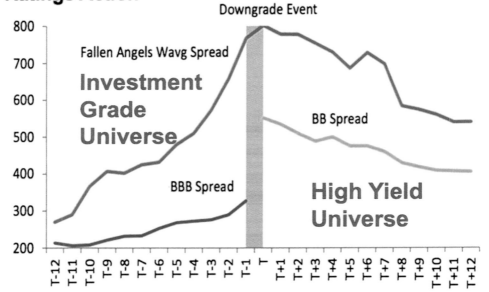

Source: Business Insider

**Prompt: Discuss fallen angels spread evolution before and after ratings action. Give a specific real-world example.**

Claude:

A real-world example is Ford Motor Company, which was downgraded to high yield by S&P and Moody's in March 2020 at the onset of the COVID pandemic and recession.

In the months leading up to the downgrades, Ford's credit spreads widened significantly as default risks grew. From January to March 2020, spreads on Ford's bonds expanded from around +100bps to over +400bps above Treasuries. The market anticipated and priced in Ford's fallen angel risk well before the actual downgrades, as spreads blew out.

Once the downgrades were officially announced, Ford's spreads tightened back in somewhat. Within a month after being cut to junk, Ford's bonds traded around +300bps over Treasuries. This reflected the removal of some uncertainty around their future trajectory after the long-expected downgrade finally occurred.

**Prompt: Expand to include why high yield funds cannot buy Ford before the downgrade even though the spread was attractive.**

Claude:
Most high yield bond funds have investment mandates that prohibit them from holding bonds rated investment grade. They can only invest in sub-IG securities.

As Ford's bonds were still technically rated IG in the months leading up to the downgrade, high yield funds were restricted from adding exposure despite the bonds trading at junk spreads. At the same time, forced selling by investment grade funds contributed to the spread widening as fallen angel risk grew. There was eager demand waiting to buy the bonds, but institutional constraints kept high yield funds sidelined.

Once Ford was formally downgraded to junk status, the restrictions were lifted. High yield funds were then able to grab the bonds at favorable spreads only after the actual downgrade occurred.

This demonstrates how mandates can create forced selling pressure ahead of technical fallen angel events unrelated to the underlying value. High yield funds sat out the widening until the downgrade triggered their ability to buy.

## Performance Comparison

The graph shows the growth of $10,000 invested in each of the securities selected for comparison. Prices adjusted for splits and dividends.

MAX 🔒   **10Y**   5Y   1Y   YTD   6M

**Prompt: How is it possible that ANGL ETF has outperformed HYG over the last 10 years?**

Claude:

There are a few potential reasons why the VanEck Vectors Fallen Angel High Yield Bond ETF (ANGL) has outperformed the iShares iBoxx High Yield Corporate Bond ETF (HYG) over the past 10 years:

Fallen angel focus - ANGL's dedicated focus on bonds originally issued as investment grade but later downgraded to high yield has provided an edge. Fallen angels have tended to outperform broad high yield post-downgrade.

**Quality bias:** ANGL's index averages BB rating versus HYG's index averaging B. ANGL's slightly higher credit quality tilt in junk may have provided better risk-adjusted returns over a decade-long period.

**Lower fees:** ANGL's expense ratio of 0.35% is lower than HYG's 0.48%, giving it a small cost advantage compounded over 10 years.

**Bond selection:** ANGL appears to have been superior at security selection within its fallen angel segment compared to HYG in the broader high yield space.

**Luck:** ANGL may have simply been "lucky" over the past 10 years as fallen angels outperformed. This pattern may not persist going forward.

| Metric | ANGL | HYG |
|---|---|---|
| Fund name | VanEck Fallen Angel High Yield Bond ETF | iShares iBoxx $ High Yield Corporate Bond ETF |
| Expense ratio | 0.35% | 0.49% |
| Assets under management | $2.83 billion | $15.92 billion |
| Average maturity | 7.2 years | 7.4 years |
| Credit quality | BBB- | BBB- |
| Yield | 5.2% | 5.0% |
| Beta | 0.67 | 0.69 |
| Sharpe ratio | 0.52 | 0.50 |

Source: Bard and Portfolio Lab

ChatGPT:

## Composition:

ANGL: ANGL has a more concentrated portfolio compared to HYG, as it primarily invests in fallen angel bonds. These bonds tend to have higher credit quality compared to typical high yield bonds, given their history as investment-grade securities.

HYG: HYG offers a more diversified approach, investing in a broad selection of high yield corporate bonds, including both newly issued high yield bonds and those that have been downgraded.

## Credit Quality:

ANGL: Due to its focus on fallen angel bonds, ANGL's portfolio may have a higher credit quality compared to the overall high yield bond market.

HYG: HYG's portfolio may have a broader credit spectrum, including lower-rated bonds, making it more representative of the entire high yield bond market.

## Performance and Risk:

ANGL: During economic recoveries, ANGL may potentially benefit from capital appreciation as the credit quality of its fallen angel bonds improves. However, it could also experience higher volatility during economic downturns due to its relatively concentrated portfolio.

HYG: HYG's broader diversification may offer more stability during market downturns, but it might have a more modest upside during economic expansions compared to ANGL.

# Chapter 10 Questions: Rating Agencies, Rising Stars and Fallen Angels:

1) What does a fallen angel bond refer to?
A) A bond downgraded from investment grade to junk status
B) A bond upgraded from junk status to investment grade
C) A bond issued by a fallen angel company
D) A bond with a fallen angel credit rating

Explanation: A is correct. A fallen angel bond is initially investment grade but later downgraded to junk status.

2) What potential conflict of interest exists with credit rating agencies?
A) They are paid by investors rather than issuers
B) They provide ratings for free to avoid any conflicts
C) They are paid by the issuers they are rating
D) They do not actually provide credit ratings

Explanation: C is correct. Rating agencies being paid by the issuers creates potential conflicts of interest.

3) What does a high debt-to-equity ratio imply about a company's credit risk?
A) Lower risk
B) Moderate risk
C) Higher risk
D) Unclear without more data

Explanation: C is correct. High financial leverage, as shown by a high D/E ratio, increases default risk.

4) During a recession, what typically happens to speculative grade default rates?
A) They decline rapidly
B) They increase
C) They are relatively unchanged
D) The impact depends on monetary policy

Explanation: B is correct. Recessions tend to increase default rates for speculative grade debt.

5) How did bond investors likely react as the Fed raised rates in 2018?
A) They upgraded bond ratings
B) They priced in higher downgrade risk
C) They focused only on economic data
D) They ignored the potential impact

Explanation: B is correct. Investors anticipated rate hikes would pressure bond ratings.

6) What does a rising star bond refer to?
A) A bond upgraded from junk status to investment grade
B) A bond downgraded from investment grade to junk status
C) A bond issued by a rising star company
D) A bond with a rising star credit rating

Explanation: A is correct. A rising star bond is upgraded from high yield to investment grade.


7) What is a potential advantage of an ETF focused on fallen angel bonds?
A) Broad diversification
B) Higher credit quality
C) Lower volatility
D) International bond exposure

Explanation: B is correct. Fallen angel ETFs can have a higher average credit rating than broad high yield ETFs.

8) How might high yield bond funds react to a potential "fallen angel" bond?
A) They cannot buy it until after the downgrade
B) They are eager to buy it on the downgrade news
C) They can buy it at any time
D) They are prohibited from ever buying it

Explanation: A is correct. High yield funds are restricted from buying bonds rated investment grade.

9) Which factor contributed to surging fallen angels in 2020?
A) Global trade tensions
B) Energy market disruptions
C) COVID-19 recession
D) Dovish monetary policy

Explanation: C is correct. The COVID recession pushed many issuers into high yield status.

10) What is a risk in relying solely on rating agencies for downgrade alerts?
A) Getting insider information
B) Acting too quickly
C) Missing early warning signs
D) Chasing unsustainable yields

Explanation: C is correct. Investors may miss early signals of credit deterioration if relying only on delayed agency actions.

11) How did Ford Motor Company's bond spreads behave after its 2020 downgrade?
A) They increased further
B) They remained stable
C) They narrowed in
D) The impact depended on maturity

Explanation: C is correct. Ford's spreads tightened after the actual junk downgrade occurred.


12) Which types of securities frequently rely on credit ratings from agencies?
A) Common stocks
B) U.S. Treasuries
C) Asset-backed securities
D) Cryptocurrencies

Explanation: C is correct. Structured securities like asset-backed and mortgage bonds often require agency ratings.

# Chapter 11 – Corporate Bonds – Bankruptcy

Bankruptcy is one of the most critical risks associated with investing in corporate bonds. When a company becomes insolvent or unable to service its debt obligations, it can seek protection through bankruptcy proceedings. For corporate bond holders, this can mean delayed payments, reduced principal, or even total loss of investment. Thus, understanding the various forms of bankruptcy and their implications is essential for managing exposure to distressed and defaulting issuers.

## Bankruptcy and Creditor Rights

Bankruptcy Reform Act of 1978
- Law which governs bankruptcy in the United States.

**Chapter 7**
- **Deals with the liquidation of a company.**

Chapter 11
- Deals with the reorganization of a company.

### Chapter 7 Bankruptcy (Liquidation):

In Chapter 7 bankruptcy, a distressed company's assets are liquidated to repay its creditors, including bondholders. When a company goes through Chapter 7, the corporate bondholders become creditors in the liquidation process. However, since secured creditors are prioritized, unsecured bondholders may recover less or even nothing from the liquidation of assets.

### Chapter 11 Bankruptcy (Reorganization):

Chapter 11 bankruptcy is commonly used by corporations to reorganize their finances and operations. During Chapter 11, the company seeks approval from bondholders for its reorganization plan, which may involve modifying the terms of existing corporate bonds or issuing new bonds. Bondholders often play a crucial role in approving or rejecting the company's restructuring proposals.

## Impact on Bondholders:

The type of bankruptcy a company files affects how bondholders' interests are treated. In Chapter 7, bondholders are typically at a greater risk of losing their investments, especially if they hold unsecured bonds. In contrast, Chapter 11 allows companies to continue their operations and provides a chance for bondholders to receive a portion of their principal and interest payments if the company successfully restructures.

## Credit Risk:

When a company faces bankruptcy or defaults on its obligations, the credit risk of its corporate bonds increases. Credit rating agencies may downgrade the bond's credit rating, signaling higher risk and potentially leading to a decline in the bond's market value.

## Default rate vs high-yield spreads

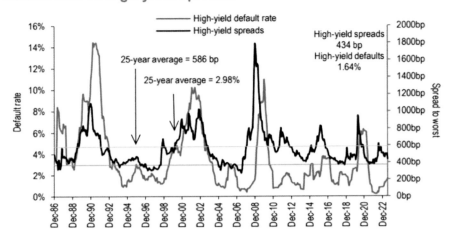

Source: J.P. Morgan; Moody's Investors Service.; Bloomberg Finance L.P.; S&P/
IHSMarkit.
Note: Default rate is par-weighted

Over the 25 years, the average spread has exceeded the default rate by about 3%. This suggests
that over a long time period, high-yield investors have obtained excess returns above just
compensation for credit losses.

As you can see in the graph above, the default rate spiked to about 12% in 2009 during the
global financial crisis, well above the 25-year average of 2.98%. This massive spike in defaults
reflects the severe economic and market turmoil during the crisis. The default rate then fell back
to below 3% by 2014 along with the economic rebound and easy financial conditions provided
by accommodative central bank policies. The decline in defaults aligned with recovering growth
and risk appetites.

To summarize, the excess spread demonstrates that high yield bonds have delivered returns
above just default compensation over time. But defaults remain cyclical, as evidenced by the
extreme spike during the financial crisis and subsequent decline during the recovery.

## Default rates by industry

| | 2020 | 2021 | 2022 | LTM | 21-yr Avg. |
|---|---|---|---|---|---|
| Automotive | 1.14% | 0.00% | 0.46% | 0.00% | 3.03% |
| Broadcasting | 0.00% | 0.00% | 0.00% | 13.34% | 2.46% |
| Cable/Satellite | 12.88% | 0.00% | 0.00% | 0.00% | 3.55% |
| Chemicals | 0.00% | 0.00% | 3.11% | 1.76% | 1.68% |
| Consumer Products | 0.00% | 0.00% | 1.39% | 0.00% | 1.79% |
| Diversified Media | 7.85% | 0.00% | 0.00% | 0.00% | 6.50% |
| Energy | 19.42% | 0.68% | 0.77% | 0.58% | 3.10% |
| Financial | 1.52% | 0.68% | 0.00% | 0.00% | 3.28% |
| Food/Beverages | 1.93% | 0.00% | 0.00% | 0.00% | 1.14% |
| Gaming/Lodging/Leisure | 0.73% | 0.00% | 0.00% | 0.55% | 2.33% |
| Healthcare | 1.93% | 0.00% | 4.26% | 6.17% | 1.00% |
| Housing | 2.34% | 0.00% | 0.00% | 0.00% | 1.17% |
| Industrials | 0.32% | 0.00% | 0.00% | 4.66% | 0.79% |
| Metals and Mining | 1.33% | 0.00% | 0.00% | 0.74% | 2.72% |
| Paper/Packaging | 0.00% | 0.00% | 0.00% | 0.00% | 2.16% |
| Retail | 14.76% | 0.00% | 0.00% | 4.53% | 2.61% |
| Services | 4.11% | 1.23% | 0.00% | 0.00% | 1.10% |
| Technology | 0.00% | 0.01% | 0.00% | 2.39% | 0.97% |
| Telecommunications | 20.30% | 0.79% | 0.00% | 0.00% | 3.77% |
| Transportation | 0.00% | 1.29% | 0.00% | 0.00% | 4.31% |
| Utility | 0.00% | 0.00% | 7.60% | 0.00% | 5.73% |
| **HY Default Rate** | 6.17% | 0.27% | 0.84% | 1.64% | 2.61% |
| Ex-Energy | 3.94% | 0.21% | 0.85% | 1.78% | 2.42% |

Source: J.P. Morgan; PitchBook Data, Inc; Bloomberg Finance L.P.
Note: Twenty-one-year average is as of December 30, 2022

As shown in the table above, the 21-year average default rate across all industries is 2.61%. Within this same time period, diversified media has recorded a 6.50% default rate while the industrial sector suffered a much lower 0.79% default rate.

Not shown in this chart, it is noteworthy that:

Media and auto sector defaults spiked above 25% in 2009 given severe demand destruction during the global financial crisis. Energy and metals also saw escalated default rates in 2015-2016 during the commodity downturn. The consumer sector has been relatively stable, though still demonstrating a cyclical pattern.

## Default rate: by rating 12 months prior to default

|  | 2020 | 2021 | 2022 | LTM | 21-yr Avg. |
|---|---|---|---|---|---|
| BB | 0.04% | 0.00% | 0.00% | 0.00% | 0.40% |
| B | 4.89% | 0.18% | 0.47% | 0.75% | 2.14% |
| CCC/Split CCC | 21.81% | 0.61% | 4.03% | 8.29% | 6.17% |
| HY Default rate | 6.17% | 0.27% | 0.84% | 1.64% | 2.61% |

Source: J.P. Morgan; PitchBook Data, Inc; Bloomberg Finance L.P.
Note: Twenty-one-year average is as of December 30, 2022

## Default rate: by rating at issuance

|  | 2020 | 2021 | 2022 | LTM | 21-yr Avg. |
|---|---|---|---|---|---|
| BB | 6.01% | 0.00% | 0.00% | 1.17% | 1.06% |
| B | 7.42% | 0.23% | 0.79% | 0.90% | 2.81% |
| CCC/Split CCC | 7.71% | 0.34% | 3.88% | 6.57% | 5.25% |
| HY Default rate | 6.17% | 0.27% | 0.84% | 1.64% | 2.61% |

Source: J.P. Morgan; PitchBook Data, Inc; Bloomberg Finance L.P.
Note: Twenty-one-year average is as of December 30, 2022

As expected, lower credit quality corresponds with higher default rates across high yield. In 2009 during the global financial crisis, default rates spiked across all rating segments, but the lower the credit quality, the higher the level of defaults:

- Bonds rated CCC/C saw default rates above 30% in 2009.
- For B-rated bonds, 2009 default rates exceeded 15%.
- Higher BB-rated bonds had default rates around 5%.
- The highest quality BBB investment grade bonds had minimal defaults.

# Bond issuer-weighted recovery rates

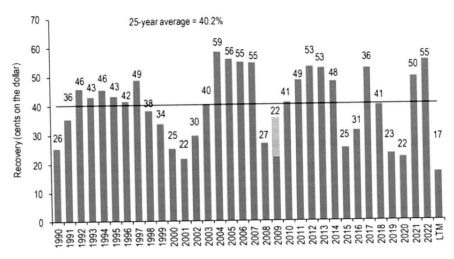

Source: J.P. Morgan; PitchBook Data, Inc.; Bloomberg Finance L.P.; Moody's Investors Service.

This chart demonstrates that despite defaults, bondholders often recover meaningful portion of value. Over this 25-year time horizon, the average recovery rate was 40.2%. This means that when a high-yield bond issuer files for bankruptcy and is liquidated, the bond holder does not lose 100%.

Bond holders get to receive the proceeds from the firm when it liquidates all its assets; they stand in line ahead of the common shareholders.

**The rate of return = Distribution Yield – Default Rate + Recovery Rate**

If a high-yield bond is yielding 10%, the default rate is 3%, and the recovery rate is 40%, then the investor rate of return is:

10% - 3% + (3% x 0.4)

Which equals:

10% - 3% + 1.2% = 8.2%

# High-yield bond default and recovery rates

| | Default Rate | Recovery rates | | | | |
|---|---|---|---|---|---|---|
| | | All Bonds | Snr Sec | Snr Unsec | Snr Sub | Sub |
| 2013 | 0.7% | 52.7 | 59.6 | 36.5 | 46.0 | 1.0 |
| 2014 | 2.9% | 48.0 | 67.7 | 31.2 | 33.8 | na |
| 2015 | 1.8% | 25.2 | 32.7 | 16.6 | 13.0 | na |
| 2016 | 3.6% | 31.1 | 36.7 | 23.2 | 0.5 | na |
| 2017 | 1.3% | 52.6 | 61.6 | 39.2 | na | na |
| 2018 | 1.8% | 39.8 | 46.3 | 32.9 | 18.0 | na |
| 2019 | 2.6% | 23.2 | 43.0 | 15.5 | na | 79.8 |
| 2020 | 6.2% | 22.0 | 43.8 | 13.8 | 19.2 | na |
| 2021 | 0.3% | 49.6 | 50.5 | 49.1 | na | na |
| 2022 | 0.8% | 55.3 | 76.8 | 45.2 | na | na |
| LTM | 1.5% | 16.8 | 33.7 | 3.9 | na | na |
| 25-yr ann. avg. | 3.0% | 40.20 | 53.01 | 35.26 | 27.18 | 31.66 |

Source: .P. Morgan; PitchBook Data, Inc.; Bloomberg Finance L.P.
Notes: Recovery rates are issuer-weighted and based on price 30 days after default date. 2009 Adj. recoveries are based on year-end prices.

This table shows importance of seniority structure for potential recovery in default scenario.

As expected, senior secured debt has highest recovery rates, averaging 53%.

Senior unsecured bonds recover around 35% on average through cycles.

Senior subordinate and subordinated bonds have lowest priority and recoveries, but still average 20-30%.

# Cumulative recovery rates by industry (2008 - YTD)

| | All Bonds | First-Lien Loan | All Loans | Senior Secured | Senior |
|---|---|---|---|---|---|
| Automotive | 59.4 | 50.0 | 43.1 | 60.3 | - |
| Broadcasting | 35.1 | 61.0 | 52.5 | 53.8 | 15.4 |
| Cable and Satellite | 66.2 | 79.5 | 79.3 | 68.0 | 48.1 |
| Chemicals | 41.8 | 53.2 | 49.6 | 48.6 | 17.3 |
| Consumer Products | 34.4 | 48.0 | 41.8 | 67.6 | 23.6 |
| Diversified Media | 29.1 | 48.0 | 45.0 | 39.3 | 33.5 |
| Energy | 29.5 | 57.7 | 52.9 | 43.4 | 28.3 |
| Financial | 32.1 | 53.6 | 52.3 | 35.3 | 32.0 |
| Food and Beverages | 23.7 | 53.7 | 51.5 | 58.8 | 23.0 |
| Gaming Lodging & Leisure | 32.1 | 60.0 | 55.8 | 28.6 | 41.8 |
| Healthcare | 36.4 | 62.5 | 55.2 | 42.7 | 56.9 |
| Housing | 36.5 | 54.0 | 48.5 | 102.5 | 32.0 |
| Industrials | 31.6 | 63.6 | 59.4 | 42.6 | 22.5 |
| Metals and Mining | 27.2 | 44.6 | 44.3 | 36.2 | 22.6 |
| Paper & Packaging | 34.8 | 63.2 | 57.8 | 50.8 | 26.6 |
| Retail | 36.8 | 45.6 | 41.1 | 60.2 | 29.8 |
| Services | 41.8 | 64.3 | 57.4 | 63.9 | 14.9 |
| Technology | 36.5 | 49.1 | 40.5 | 44.2 | 7.3 |
| Telecommunications | 32.4 | 68.8 | 68.2 | 44.2 | 9.0 |
| Transportation | 30.3 | 47.1 | 47.1 | 37.8 | 22.4 |
| Utility | 67.8 | 64.7 | 55.7 | 73.4 | 51.9 |
| Total | 33.5 | 54.7 | 50.5 | 47.0 | 29.0 |

Source: J.P. Morgan; PitchBook Data, Inc.; Bloomberg Finance L.P.; S&P/IHSMarkit.

## US Recovery Rates by Industry

The cable/satellite and utilities sectors have historically maintained the highest corporate bond recovery rates, often exceeding 60%, for a few key reasons:

Substantial tangible assets: These companies own extensive infrastructure assets including transmission lines, satellites, cable systems, power plants etc. These retain significant value even in distress.

Predictable cash flows: Their revenue streams from customers paying monthly bills are more stable and predictable than other industries. This supports ongoing operations in bankruptcy.

Monopoly/oligopoly structures: As concentrated marketplaces with high barriers to entry, distressed firms maintain customer bases and pricing power. Regional utilities in particular approach monopolies.

Regulation: Government oversight bodies like public utility commissions help shield utilities from more severe distress. The regulated structure aids recoveries.

Critical services: Cable/satellite TV and utility services are considered necessities with inelastic demand. Customers rarely stop paying bills altogether.

There are a few factors that contribute to the food and beverage sector typically having the lowest corporate bond recovery rates, averaging around 23%:

Low tangible asset values: Food/beverage companies operate with lower fixed asset investments compared to capital intensive sectors. This limits collateral value in distress.

Commodity input costs: Variable costs of agricultural commodities and raw ingredients lead to lower profit margins and less cushion in downturns.

Fragmented competition: The industry is highly competitive with low barriers to entry, making it difficult to sustain pricing power in bankruptcy.

Perishable inventories: Inventories like fresh foods and beverages have little recovery value given short shelf lives that render stock obsolete quickly.

Consumer discretionary nature - Demand for non-essential food/beverage products sees sharper declines in recessions relative to staples.

Low margins/high leverage - Many operators run on thin margins and high debt loads, leaving little equity buffer in bankruptcy.

In between these extremes, even lower recovery industries still see bondholders getting 25-45% back post-default.

# Chapter 10 Questions: Corporate Bonds - Bankruptcy:

1) What happens to a distressed company's assets in Chapter 7 bankruptcy?

A) They are reorganized

B) They are liquidated

C) They are sold to creditors

D) They are transferred to shareholders

Explanation: B is correct. In Chapter 7 bankruptcy, the company's assets are liquidated to pay off creditors.

2) How are bondholders typically impacted if a company files for Chapter 7 bankruptcy?

A) They are given priority payouts over common shareholders

B) They lose all their investments

C) They vote on the reorganization plan

D) Their bonds are converted to common shares

Explanation: A is correct. Common shareholders are the last to be paid

3) What is the purpose of Chapter 11 bankruptcy for corporations?

A) To shut down operations

B) To renegotiate with shareholders

C) To liquidate assets

D) To reorganize finances and operations

Explanation: D is correct. Chapter 11 allows corporations to restructure and reorganize.

4) Which type of bankruptcy filing allows bondholders to vote on a restructuring plan?

A) Chapter 7

B) Chapter 13

C) Chapter 11

D) Chapter 15

Explanation: C is correct. Bondholders can vote on corporate reorganization plans in Chapter 11.

5) How did speculative grade bond default rates behave during the 2008-09 financial crisis?

A) They declined rapidly

B) They increased slightly

C) They were relatively stable

D) They spiked significantly

Explanation: D is correct. Speculative grade default rates surged during the 2008-09 crisis.

6) According to the data, which credit rating category had the highest default rate in 2009?

A) AAA

B) BB

C) B

D) CCC/C

Explanation: D is correct. The lowest CCC/C category had the highest 2009 default rates exceeding 30%.

7) Which sector has historically had the highest average default rate over 21 years?

A) Consumer goods

B) Industrial

C) Technology

D) Media

Explanation: D is correct. Diversified media recorded the highest average default rate of 6.5% based on the data.

8) What does a high recovery rate indicate for corporate bondholders?

A) Their priority in bankruptcy claims

B) A lower return of principal

C) Higher potential investment losses

D) A higher return of principal

Explanation: D is correct. High recovery rates mean bondholders receive a greater portion of principal back.

9) What was the average high yield bond recovery rate over 25 years?

A) 1%

B) 10%

C) 40%

D) 90%

Explanation: C is correct. The data showed an average high yield bond recovery rate of 40.2% over 25 years.

10) Where do corporate bondholders typically rank in priority for bankruptcy claims?

A) Senior to shareholders

B) Senior to secured creditors

C) Junior to shareholders

D) Junior to secured creditors

Explanation: A is correct. Bondholders have higher seniority than shareholders but lower than secured creditors.

11) Which sector has historically had the highest recovery rates?

A) Transportation

B) Food and beverage

C) Utilities

D) Technology

Explanation: C is correct. The utility sector has averaged the highest recovery rates.

12) Which types of assets help contribute to high recovery rates for cable/satellite companies?

A) Transmission lines and power plants

B) Inventories and warehouses

C) Infrastructure and predictable cash flows

D) Factories and equipment

Explanation: C is correct. Cable/satellite companies benefit from infrastructure assets and stable cash flows.

13) During an economic downturn, what typically happens to the default rate for high yield corporate bonds?

A) It remains stable

B) It increases significantly

C) It declines gradually

D) The impact depends on monetary policy

Explanation: B is correct. Recessions tend to increase default rates for below investment grade debt.

14) What factor contributes to low recovery rates for food and beverage companies?

A) Extensive property ownership

B) Perishable inventories

C) Regional monopolies

D) Steady demand

Explanation: B is correct. Perishable products lose value quickly and contribute to low recoveries.

15) How can investors potentially estimate returns on high yield bonds?

A) Yield + Default rate

B) Yield - Default rate + Recovery rate

C) Yield x Recovery rate

D) (Yield x Default rate) + Recovery rate

Explanation: B is correct. Expected returns equal yield minus default.

== THE END ==

Made in United States
North Haven, CT
12 September 2023

41443897R10113